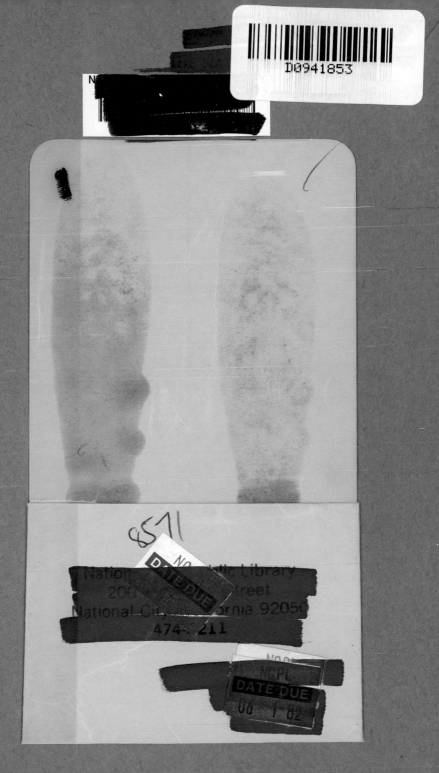

A
Dreadful
Man

BRIAN AHERNE

assisted by

George Sanders and Benita Hume

SIMON AND SCHUSTER
NEW YORK

Published by Simon and Schuster
A Division of Gulf & Western Corporation
Simon & Schuster Building
Rockefeller Center
1230 Avenue of the Americas
New York, New York 10020
Designed by Edith Fowler
Manufactured in the United States of America

1 2 3 4 5 6 7 8 9 10

Library of Congress Cataloging in Publication Data

Aherne, Brian.
   A dreadful man.

   1. Sanders, George, date.   2. Moving-
picture actors and actresses—Great Britain—
Biography.
I. Sanders, George, date.   II. Hume,
Benita.
III. Title.
PN2598.S33A63   791.43'028'0924 [B]   79-10513
ISBN 0-671-24797-2

For My Wife
and
For My Friends
Known and Unknown

---

*All the events described in this story are true,
but in some cases names have been changed
out of deference to personal or family feelings.*

B.A.

1

BARCELONA, SPAIN. *April 25, 1972 (UPI).*

British movie actor George Sanders, 65, died today in a resort hotel here, apparently from an overdose of sleeping pills, according to the official Spanish news agency CIFRA, leaving behind a suicide note which read, "I am committing suicide because I am bored. I feel I have lived long enough. I leave you all in your sweet little cesspool and I wish you luck." Five empty bottles of Nembutal were found in his room.

How is it possible, one may ask, that a man still not old by modern standards, still successful in his profession, in fair physical health, possessed of adequate means, well educated, highly intelligent and brilliantly talented in many ways should so lack courage, so lack interest in all that life has to offer, that he could find no other course open to him but death? Are there not fine things to be done in the world, wrongs to be righted, peaks to be climbed, suffering to be helped, lessons to be learned? Could he find nothing to enjoy? Was he unmoved by the glories of the sky, the dawn and the sunset, the recurrent miracle of the changing seasons, the interest and beauty of a garden and the silent mystery of wild life? Was he blind to the art and literature, deaf to the music created by mankind through the ages? Did he derive no comfort from his family and friends? Is it possible that such a man could tamely succumb to the ignominy of boredom?

Yes, it is possible. In fact, it was inevitable.

I was George Sanders' friend for many years. He had one other, Stuart Hall, his stand-in, secretary, nurse and steadfast ill-used companion throughout his life in Hollywood. I once asked this remarkable man why we were both willing to be George's friends, because, I said, I suspected that he was not really capable of friendship and in the eyes of others he was a dreadful man.

Stuart thought this over for a moment and then replied, "Well, speaking for myself, I would say that I am his friend because, even when he goes off into those interminable silences, the son of a bitch *never bores me,* and frankly most people do!"

I agreed with him, but he and I were speaking as Englishmen of the "old school," whereas George was really a Slav, having been born in St. Petersburg of Russian parents who claimed British descent. In his autobiography, George says, "It was from forebears of solid social position and impeccable respectability that my mother came. To the best of my knowledge, my father came in the mail." However, in a recent letter his sister, Margaret, says, "I have only just discovered that Tom, George and I were fed a lot of baloney by our parents as to our father's real background. It appears that Sanders is an assumed name only and our father was, in reality, the illegitimate son of a Prince von Oldenburg and a very beautiful Russian Countess whose name I have been so far unable to discover. The Prince was married to one of the Czar's sisters, and I have a medallion with two crowns, one blue and one scarlet, and entwined initials. It's a long story and full of gaps—everybody is too old to remember details."

It was always evident to me that his Slavic blood predominated, so that he was never really at ease with Anglo-Saxons, to whom his behavior seemed as peculiar, and often as boorish, as that of some Russian political figures of today. It has been my personal impression, however, that the Celts get along better than the Anglo-Saxons with the introverted, difficult Slavs, so it is possible that my Irish blood enabled me to be amused rather than insulted.

The interminable silences that Stuart Hall mentioned did not disturb me at all, because, in an odd way, they were never empty: I was always aware that George was thinking and would eventually produce some unusual idea that would amuse me. He had no small talk, being totally uninterested in gossip or chat about personalities—and this would infuriate many hostesses and the unfortunate ladies who were placed next to him at dinner—but national or international affairs or, best of all, a philosophic discussion would arouse him, and then he would express opinions which often delighted me by their originality and impracticality. I knew too that he was capable of genuine kindness and compassion, though this was a side of his nature that others rarely saw.

In his autobiography, *Memoirs of a Professional Cad*, George describes the day on which his mother took him to school in England and says:

I remember having an odd feeling on the day we left St. Petersburg that we would never return. As it turned out, we never did. It was this poignant moment of leave-taking that was also my closest brush with history. Sir Winston Churchill touched unwittingly on it when he wrote of certain events which were taking place in 1917:

In the middle of April the Germans took a sombre decision—they turned upon Russia the most grisly of all weapons. They transported Lenin, in a sealed truck, like a plague bacillus from Switzerland into Russia.

Lenin was going in as I was going out. At the Finland Station in St. Petersburg he was being met by his pals Joe Stalin, Kamenev, Zinoviev, Trotsky and the rest of the Bolshevik gangsters. I was being seen off by my father, my uncle Frederick in his scarlet Cossack uniform, my Aunt Margaret, Prince and Princess Erivansky, Count Beckendorff and my Cousin Agnes. Lenin was arriving full of plans for my money. I was leaving for school in England, serenely unaware of his existence. To the rest of our gay and well-to-do gathering, Lenin and his fellow conspirators were just a bunch of rather badly behaved peasants. Lenin's plans were not confined to the appropriation of the various trust funds that affluent uncles and aunts of mine had set up to insure for me the sort of life that would have suited my indolent nature—they were far more comprehensive, including everybody else's money as well. They also included the murder of most of my relatives.

I must confess that there are times when I wish they had included the murder of all of them: however, I think I might have spared the ones who provided for me. Quite frankly, I am sorry about that money. I would have liked to have had it.

No one took any notice of the fact that on April 2, 1917, President Wilson spoke of "the wonderful and heartening things that have been happening in the last few weeks in Russia." American sentiment was solidly on the side of the revolutionaries. The very next day, April 3rd, Kerensky's provisional government was granted credits by the U.S.A. amounting to $325,000,000. For this modest sum America not only guaranteed the success of the revolution, she also bought herself a lifelong enemy, to defend herself against whom it has cost her untold billions of dollars and a tax burden as onerous as that of 1776. The Czar certainly had at his disposal the means with which to subdue the revolutionaries. But he didn't have the heart [or the brain? —B.A.]

At Brighton College in England, George must have had a hard time, for in those days middle-class British schoolboys could be very cruel to foreigners, whom they regarded as "frogs," "wops," "dagoes" and so on. Conscious of his superior breeding, talents and intelligence, he withdrew behind a protective mask, compounded of shyness and intellectual contempt, and thus formed the personality which was later to intrigue audiences on the screen. When at last his school days were over, he got, through some connection of his mother's, a job with a cigarette manufacturing company in the Argentine. George was sent as a sort of public relations man down to the wilds of Patagonia, where he was supposed to convert the native and isolated sheepherders to the company's brands. It was an impossible task, but he was young and enjoyed the open air life, spending his days in the saddle, eating and sleeping around a campfire under the brilliant stars, and learning to speak Spanish and play the guitar. The company finally awoke to the fact that he was doing no business and sent Sanders off to try his luck in Chile, where, as he delighted to relate, he became the guest of a charming lady in her comfortable villa.

Unfortunately George's nights were disturbed by the lady's jealous fiancé, who would bang on the shutters and shout Spanish curses outside. One night, both George and the fiancé being very drunk, George threw open the shutters and shouted back, whereupon the fiancé reeled out of the darkness and presented two pistols, challenging him to a duel. George grabbed one, fell out of the window somehow and staggered into the darkness of the garden. There these two intoxicated boys—for they were no more—lost each other for a time. Being barefooted, George made no noise when he moved, but he could hear his rival's footsteps on the gravel, and when they stopped he fired in that direction. There was a grunt and the sound of a falling body. The lady emerged with a lantern and, seeing her fiancé lying in what seemed to be a pool of blood, she screamed and rushed to telephone a doctor, difficult to find at that time of the night. Anyway, the operator became so alarmed at what she heard on the line that she called the police, and George spent the rest of the night in the local jail.

Next day the company sent a man down who did whatever was necessary in Chile to set George free, and this was a relief, because there was a boy in the jail with him who had been there for eighteen months awaiting trial for stealing a piece of cheese. "When I say they set me free," said George, "I mean just that, because they threw me not only out of the company but out of South America."

2

In the aftermath of World War I hundreds of thousands of young men were discharged from the British armed forces with no jobs, no training for anything but warfare, and nothing but a small "gratuity" in their pockets. Some of these took advantage of the government's widely advertised offer to provide free or assisted passages and grants of land to those who would emigrate to Kenya, Rhodesia or similar colonies. There they brought peace to the eternally warring tribes, cleared the bush, drained the swamps, made the deserts blossom and established civilization, law and justice where only ignorance, darkness and degradation reigned before. I believe that those who are still alive and their descendants have cause to feel bitter about the perfidy of politicians who now treat their own kith and kin as enemies.

Many "demobed" soldiers who remained in Britain had difficulty surviving. The tide of history had swept over them, and the next generation, who couldn't care less, were pouring in. Sometime in the twenties, I can remember stopping to look at a fine figure of a man dressed in the civvy suit, now threadbare, issued by the Army at the time of demobilization, standing in the gutter of Regent Street in London, holding a card on which he had written that he was a former major in a famous regiment who had spent three years on active service in France and it listed his decorations. In his other hand he held a little tray with a few pencils on it which he hoped to sell in order to get something to eat. I had no need of a pencil, but the sight of him moved me deeply and I bought one. He thanked me in a cultivated voice. I never forgot him, but there were many like him.

It was this world to which George returned from South America, with no idea of how or where he could earn a living. I was there, for we were about the same age, but it was to be some years before we met in California.

Fortunately for George, one of the great heroes of his childhood, Uncle Sasha, had arrived in London from St. Petersburg, where he had throughout the revolution indulged in one of his favorite pastimes. From his great carved bed, a .22 pistol in his hangover-shaking hand, he would shoot flies that had gathered to eat the jam he had smeared on the ceiling. Liveried footmen stood by with champagne, extra rounds of ammunition, orange marmalade and strawberry jam. Outside in the streets men were dying for a cause to which they were passionately attached but did not really understand, a cause which only specious dialectics could explain.

The reunion with George cheered Uncle Sasha, who set about teaching his errant nephew to sing. Every morning, after warming up on the scales, he made George sing "Because" again and again, Uncle insisting that it provided the finest vocal exercise. He was right, for George developed a genuine resonant baritone voice which never left him. As for Uncle Sasha, like many White Russians he became a professional house guest, until his welcome wore thin. Then he became a guest in the wrong sort of houses, until in the end he died of syphilis on the Riviera.

And so it was that George played and sang a few songs at a little unknown night club, where he was heard by a producer who offered him a job in a musical show. But, George said, he was so bad that they threw him out before it opened. Very small jobs followed in very small night clubs, until by sheer luck he was hired as Noël Coward's understudy in *Conversation Piece*, with which he subsequently went to Broadway.

Small parts in British pictures led to a 20th Century contract in Hollywood, where he demonstrated that, whatever his acting talent might be, he was one of the finest croquet players on the West Coast, the strategy of the game appealing to his mind. Indeed, he had a natural aptitude for all kinds of games, although he was too indolent to take advantage of it.

George's many and varied talents never ceased to amaze those who knew him. Noël Coward expressed our feeling when, after a small dinner party, George drifted to the piano as was his custom and played softly and with great charm—not for us, but for his own pleasure—after which he produced a guitar and sang in French, Russian and Spanish, finally playing the instrument behind his head while he sang an Argentine love song.

"Just look at that fellow!" cried Coward. "He has more talents than any of us, but he doesn't do anything with them!"

I think there is little doubt that he could have had an important career as an operatic baritone if he had wished. He once tried to convince me that I too had a voice of promise and actually induced me to follow his Uncle Sasha's advice and sing "Because" for half an hour every morning, but I'm afraid I soon tired of that. He then took me to his new teacher, Maestro Cepparo, a retired veteran of the Italian opera who lived in a crumbling old mansion on a hill in Culver City, California, where he coached the voices of Metro-Goldwyn-Mayer stars. I must say I found these lessons very enjoyable; and George, as my sponsor, would go along from time to time to monitor my progress.

One morning the maestro suggested that we start by having George sing a couple of arias by way of example to me, and this he did with the most impressive expertise. No sooner had he finished than a strange gentleman, who had evidently been listening through an open door, walked into the room. He was introduced as the manager of the San Francisco Opera Company and had been planted there by the maestro. Grasping George's hand in admiration, he invited him to sing Scarpia in *Tosca* in their forthcoming opera season!

To the amazement of Maestro Cepparo and myself, George refused this magnificent offer, quite gracefully but firmly, and in the succeeding weeks neither of us could persuade him to change his mind. He said he did not want to become an opera singer.

My own vocal training, over which George exercised such careful supervision, resulted in only one public performance, unexpected, successful, enjoyable and unpaid. This took place one moonlit evening at an open-air restaurant in the piazza of Capri where, as is the custom in Italy, a group of guitar players moved among the tables during dinner. Carried away by the romantic setting and the music, and no doubt by the Italian wine, I rose and burst into song with "Torna a Sorriento," to be greeted with cries of "Bravo!" and "Metropolitano!" I then gave them Toselli's "Serenade" and as an encore "O Sole Mio," all in Italian as I had learned them with the maestro, and sat down flushed with pride and joy.

It is possible that Maestro Cepparo might not have approved my performance, but I like to think that George would have been pleased with the result of his efforts on my behalf. Metropolitano! Well, after that I felt I had achieved my ambition and I never sang in public again.

George himself claimed that he was an electrician at heart, and he enjoyed nothing more than the chance to change all the wiring in your house, to electrify your clocks, light your paintings and bookshelves and install complicated systems by which the lights could be brightened or dimmed in your dining room. He knew all about transformers, transistors, A.C. and D.C. and such things that baffle most of us, and if the necessary equipment was not readily available he would make it, for he always had a workshop—sometimes two, one for wood and the other for metal work, both completely equipped with machinery.

I discovered another of his talents quite recently, when my wife and I drove down to lunch with his charming sister, Margaret, at her house in Sussex, England. Her note, by the way, was the classic invitation from the English lady living in the country.

LITTLE PADDOCKS
HAMPERS LANE
ST LEONARDS PARK
HORSHAM, SUSSEX

4th June '78

Dear Brian,
It occurs to me that if you are thinking of driving down, I had better let you have some instructions as to finding me.

You will presumably leave London by the Kingston Bye-Pass, turning left at the old Ace Of Spades and continuing until you get onto the A 24 through Leatherhead, Dorking etc. The A 24 brings you straight down to Horsham, and it is important that you take the *first* left turn into the town because otherwise you will land in the middle of Horsham, which has become a ghastly muddle of re-routings and one-way streets so that you would have trouble getting out of it. If you take the *first* entry you miss all this, and it is relatively simple. Proceed along this road until you reach the first traffic lights and turn left here into Hurst Road which will lead you to the little railway station. Here you turn left again, over the little railway bridge, then sharp right, *before* the bollards, at the foot of the bridge. Around the bend in the road you take the first small turning to the left, marked Depot Road, and proceed to the end. You will then see, facing you and *slightly* to the right, the beginning of Hampers Lane. After a few yards, you cross a small housing estate called Smithbarn, and you go on straight down Hampers Lane, where there is a notice saying "Private Road. Bridle-Path only." After about a mile the lane bends to the left and you pass a big Old People's Home on the left, and then there are two smaller houses, also on the left, one of which is occupied by a family of gypsies who keep horses in the big barn on the right, which used to be a riding school. Opposite this is an old and largish house, marked simply "Paddocks," and you're there. I am on the left-hand side of this house.

I need hardly say we went by train and she met us in her car.

Among the interesting things Margaret produced that day was a book, which I have before me as I write. It is quite a big book of 271 pages, written in longhand and bound, in hard covers of course, by George himself, who also executed the exterior cover design. It is all one letter to his father in England. The letter book took him several months of sporadic work and gives his impressions of Hollywood.

On the first page he says only, "Dad. Here is the delayed letter I promised you. It *must* be opened in the *evening*, in front of the fire and in the presence of the rest of the family, Mother, Tom and Margaret."

The next page contains a "List of Illustrations," some of which are his own sketches and some picture postcards. On the third page he gives firm instructions that no bills, charitable appeals or begging letters of any kind are to be forwarded to him. On the fourth page his marathon letter starts.

HERMIT'S GLEN
HOLLYWOOD

16th Oct 1937

Dear Dad,

Many thanks for your letters which are always a joy to read. I have steadfastly ignored the bills sent by Messrs Hawes & Curtis for making a "Lounge Suit" at £30, so after sending it several times they sent me a new one for $12, but I have no lounge suit by Hawes & Curtis in my wardrobe so have accepted the evident fact that this is another "bookkeeping error." Mind you, I do not blame them for trying. They have made a good deal of money out of me in the past, and now that my orders have stopped perhaps they are not altogether unjustified in assuming that with the aid of a skilled accountant they might *continue* to make money out of me without bothering to send the goods along with their bills.

For several months past I have been planning my spare time upon a set regimen. I allow myself one hour a day for concentrated meditation. One of my favourite reveries is the idea of founding an institution from which you send out bills to people all over the world, and then sue them when they don't pay. You get a commission from the lawyers your unfortunate victims employ to defend themselves.

Most people are so timid, so jealous of their reputation, or so poor that they would stump up without a murmur, and the others would be taken care of by their lawyers.

I am now getting ready to start my next picture, and that is always an odd sensation; you always wonder if it's going to be your last! Nobody knows how long their luck is going to hold in this town. Some people stay on top for years, others never get there and some get to the top and fall down to the bottom almost immediately. Even in the short time I have been here I have seen quite a few people come and go! But in the light of existing conditions I sometimes wonder if it's worthwhile *trying* to get on top if all one's savings are going to be taken away by the government. It is idle to sit around and say we are living under the threat of communism: this *is* communism! High taxation is nothing more or less than the practical application of communistic theory— everybody gets levelled out.

When you add to the various Federal and State taxes the commissions and what-not that are filched from your pay check before you get it, by parasites of the industry—the Motion Picture Relief Fund—the Community Chests— Agents, Business Managers, Public Relations men, Insurance etc, added again to the compulsory expenses such as wardrobe, transport, Premieres and so on, you are finally left with a couple of half-pennies to jingle on a tombstone.

But today's taxes are nothing compared to what is promised for tomorrow! You wait until the labor movement really gets hold of things!

I have an awful feeling that I shall become rich just about the time the whole thing is over, the hoarding of money prohibited, and that I shall be faced with the realisation that I might just as well have saved myself the trouble and sat on my backside in Leatherhead all the time.

By the way, you might tell Margaret that I had dinner with Clark Gable the other night and put in a good word for her.

The fact that Tom made an unsuccessful test should not depress him. I have made plenty of unsuccessful tests, and so has everybody else in the business. And the fact that they said Tom did not photograph well should be no cause for alarm, since they said precisely the same thing to Ronald Colman!

But whether the picture business is worth getting into or not is another matter. The amount of intrigue involved in the social life out here is often so tiresome, and the amount of restraint, diplomacy and bum-sucking that has to be done so nauseating that there are times when one asks oneself the question, "Is success worth the price you pay for it?" This is a question I hope to be able to answer in a few years time.

To give you some idea of the lengths to which people go to break into pictures—and I refer of course to subtleties and not to such practises as jumping into Producers' cars and trying to rub them up the right way. Incidentally, jumping into Producers' beds and trying to rub them up the right way has been found to be infinitely more effective by feminine aspirants— Well, as I was saying, to give you an idea of what people will do to get into pictures—a fellow called Jim Reagan had a daughter who was the apple of his eye. Naturally she wanted to break into pictures, as all daughters do at some time or other.

Now he was a crafty fellow and went about it in an interesting way. Giving up a lucrative position in an oil company, he managed to get a job as a clerk in the Government service and after four years hard work and much intrigue and shifting around he was finally appointed to the position he sought—Inspector of Income Taxes.

I need scarcely say that his daughter was immediately signed to a seven years film contract. And I need scarcely say that I am taking her out dancing.

I am happy to say that I have been spared the more arduous forms of intrigue, as generally I can sling the bull-shit faster than the other guy—but of course I am touching wood and hoping my luck will hold. The problem is to get the good parts. It is a fact beyond dispute that three bad parts in a row will ruin any actor's career, but *good* parts, which lead to greater popularity and bigger money, only occur at rare intervals, whereas bad parts occur all the time. Everybody wants to do the good parts, nobody the bad. Almost everybody eligible for the bad parts is eligible for the good, so that whoever wins, wins, and whoever loses, loses, if you see what I mean.

Preparations for my next picture *Shanghai Deadline* have not quite reached what I might call the "Hell—Lets Shoot It!" stage and consequently there are numerous story conferences, at which tremendous attention to the minutest detail of dialogue and characterisation is paid by all concerned, and advance scripts marked "Revised Temporary Final" are issued to the principals. It never pays, however, to *read* these scripts as the entire story is invariably rewritten on the set, the dialogue improvised by the players, and the characterisation moulded by the Director in accordance with his day-to-day moods, whims and fancies.

When the shooting finishes, many of the scenes are retaken, and when these retakes are cut into the picture it is trimmed, which means that most of your best lines are cut. Then they find they have over-footage and have to take large chunks out of a picture now lacerated to a point where the continuity is affected, and upon seeing which a much-befuddled audience has to go home and try to figure out why so-and-so was murdered, and why so-and-so didn't steal the pearl necklace instead of so-and-so.

Upon being cast for the part, you will probably be called to the Studio for an interview with the Producer. (In the world of the theatre, the words Producer and Director are synonymous, but in the film business the Director is the fellow who directs the picture, and his status is that of an artist, whereas the Producer is the big-shot but his function, apart from some prodigious cigar-smoking, is never quite clear.) Your scene in the Producer's office follows a more or less set routine.

You enter—you are offered a cigar, which you accept with alacrity but ask if you may smoke it later—you are offered a chair which looks comfortable but you perch on the edge of it, timorously, as would a maiden about to receive the favour of her Sovereign. The Producer will then proceed to read your scenes to you in a flat tone, punctuated by an impressive amount of throat-clearing, spitting and cigar-puffing and innumerable telephone calls. You realise that most of these lines won't even survive the "Revised" stage, let alone the "Revised Temporary Final" nonsense, and most of your dialogue is destined for the cutting room floor. You must keep awake and alert however, in order to play your part in the following dialogue which ensues:

PRODUCER—with the air of one about to receive the compliment of a lifetime.

"Well—what do you think of the story, eh?"

YOU—in accordance with the best rules of diplomacy, with emphasis but committing yourself to nothing.

"WHAT DO I THINK OF THE STORY????!!!!!!"

PRODUCER—with a chuckle.

"I knew you'd like it!"

YOU—trying to get as many expressions into your face as possible at the same time.

"OH!!! MR. WURTZELHEIMER!!!!!!!!!!

You leave, feeling that perhaps a blow has been struck by somebody for something or other, if only to promote better understanding between Producer and Produced: at least it provides the former with the salutary, if erroneous, illusion that he is working for his living.

Few people outside his Studio saw George in those days. He seemed to live a solitary and monastic life, and even after he married a girl named Elsie, whom he met on the set, he did not change his ways. He brought her to my house in Beverly Hills one evening and announced that as he could not stand the name of Elsie he had changed it to Susan. As I remember, she was a quiet, timid little soul and spoke little. Some time later, when he made one of his rare appearances at a Hollywood party, I asked where Susan was.

"Oh, I can't bring her," he replied. "She bores people."

He designed and built a house, furnishing it himself and not allowing Susan to see it until it was finished. After being shown around, she was reported to have said, "Oh, I'm such a lucky girl to be married to such a wonderful man!" I am afraid poor Susan didn't last long.

When the war broke out in 1939, the "British Colony," as it was known in Hollywood, plunged into all kinds of public activities in support of the British cause. The British War Relief Association, Bundles for Britain and other organizations were formed, collecting money and supplies which were shipped to England. To these we became heavy subscribers, and we traveled back and forth across the U.S. making speeches and public appearances. After America's entry into the war in 1941, we worked hard visiting Army camps and hospitals, selling War Bonds at huge rallies all over the country, and going to far corners of the world to entertain and comfort the boys in the armed forces. George did none of these things, and seemed to feel none of the patriotic fervor which gripped us. He was attacked about his attitude at a cocktail party by Nigel Bruce, who demanded to know the reason. George downed his drink, took a pull at his cigarette, and replied calmly, "Because I am a shit!"

England was not home to him, as it was to us, but merely a country in which he had spent some unhappy years as a refugee, and he continued to tinker in his workshop and sneer his way through pictures, becoming very unpopular locally in consequence. We saw little of him for some years. When he formed a liaison with Zsa Zsa Gabor, however, he came back into our lives.

George seems to have retained his power over women all his life. "A woman, a dog and a walnut tree: the more you beat 'em, the better they be," he used to quote, and there is no doubt they seemed to love it: even the witty and spirited Zsa Zsa loved it, despite the beating she took. They had been living together for some time when circumstances impelled them to get married, which they did in Las Vegas. Zsa Zsa relates that they took a taxi from the airport and drove down the main street until they saw a sign proclaiming:

GET MARRIED IN 15 MINUTES
FEE $25.00

George said that would do, so they went in, signed the papers and paid the twenty-five dollars. When the unblushing bride came out, she found her new husband had made no hotel reservations and the best they could get was a room in a motel for the night. It was sparsely furnished with a bed, a dressing table and one armchair. George immediately sat in the chair, so Zsa Zsa sat on the bed.

"Neither of us spoke," says Zsa Zsa. "George was thinking of his lost freedom and I was thinking of my lost alimony!"

The following day they returned to George's apartment on Sunset Boulevard in Hollywood, which consisted of a living room, a tiny kitchen, one bedroom and a bathroom, while below this was an enormous workshop equipped with all George's lathes, presses and tools. As Zsa Zsa had a three-year-old daughter and a nurse for her, she rightly complained that there was not enough space for the family. She said they must have a house, but George would not be budged from his workshop.

Hunting around, the bride found a suitable and charming house in Bel Air, and with great difficulty George was at last persuaded to look at it. He liked it very much and advised her to buy it. But, asked Zsa Zsa, was he not going to buy it for her? Of course he had no such intention. Conrad Hilton had given her an adequate sum of money on their divorce, he said, and if she wanted a house she should pay for it; as for himself, he already had an apartment!

In great distress, Zsa Zsa ran to her friends. What did we think of such conduct on the part of her new husband? she tearfully asked. We could only answer that it was no more than we expected, and, after all, she had had plenty of time to know him before marriage, but love is blind. In the end, she bought the house.

Several months later, after decorating and furnishing, Zsa Zsa moved into their new home, and that evening George arrived carrying in one hand a small overnight case and in the other a suit and clean shirt on a hanger. He soon established a daily custom of enjoying a swim in her pool before he departed for his workshop, returning only in time for dinner. He paid not a penny toward the upkeep of the home, claiming that as it was Zsa Zsa's house it was up to her to maintain it. Their married life was stormy, to say the least, and provided us all with much interest and no little hilarity.

It was no surprise to anyone when Zsa Zsa launched upon an acting career, at first on the radio, then on the screen and later on television. With her wit, beauty, and irrepressible gaiety, she soon began to be successful. George was very put out about this and became petulant, for he had not envisaged the possibility of two stars in the home. His remarks were not encouraging, but Zsa Zsa pressed on—and continued to love him.

About this time Mama Gabor, having heard George sing, conceived the idea that he should follow Ezio Pinza, the great Metropolitan Opera baritone, in the leading part opposite Mary Martin in *South Pacific;* and George, who was going through a lean spell in Hollywood, saw a chance to escape from the shadow of his spirited and successful wife and embark on a new career. He would admit to no enthusiasm, affecting always to despise the craft of acting, but he made preparations in his usual devious way. Hour after hour, day after day, he listened to Pinza's record and sang "Some Enchanted Evening" until Stuart and I begged him to desist, because he had nothing to fear. He then hired the biggest and best equipped recording stage in Hollywood, at Universal Studios, for one day and engaged an orchestra to accompany him, all at a cost of $2500. When he heard the record, he was not pleased with the orchestration, so he did the whole thing over again a couple of weeks later: total cost, $5000, a considerable sum for a record in those days. He mailed it to Rodgers and Hammerstein in New York, with no comment. A few days later they telephoned him in great excitement, hardly able to believe what they had heard. Would he be willing to come East and sing for them on the stage? they asked. Calmly he did so, and returned with a contract for the balance of the run of the show in his pocket. The Gabor family, Stuart and myself and the few others to whom the doings of George were a private delight were proud and happy for him. We had no doubt that he would stun the Broadway world, as he had Rodgers and Hammerstein.

A couple of weeks later, he phoned me. "Brian," he said in a conspiratorial voice, "I want to ask you something."

"Yes, George?"

There followed one of the long silences for which he was well known. I bore it for a few minutes and then I said, "Are you there, George?"

"Yes." Another silence, and then slowly he asked, "Do you think I can do it?"

"Do what? Oh—*South Pacific?* Of course you can do it! You are perfect casting and they are lucky to get you. Now don't worry! You may find the first night nerve-racking because you are not accustomed to the stage; but we all feel the same, and you will soon get over that, I promise you."

"It's not the first night I am worrying about," he said irritably. "It's the twenty-first! I couldn't last that long!"

I tried to reassure him, but soon after he produced a doctor's certificate testifying that he was suffering from an acute backache that would prevent his appearance, armed with which he persuaded Rodgers and Hammerstein to release him from the contract. At about the same time, he went into psychiatry, and, after defeating five eminent practitioners within two years, he found one who, he claimed, had transformed him.

"In what way, George?" I asked.

"Well, look at me!" he said testily. "Don't you *see* the difference?"

I couldn't honestly say that I did, but by that time I had acquired an amused affection for this crusty, eccentric character, and I would have been sorry to see him change. However, the result of all this psychiatry was that he became convinced that he must separate from Zsa Zsa. "I *must* get out of this ridiculous marriage in which I have got myself involved!" he would groan, and he now spent most of his time at his apartment.

In the meantime Zsa Zsa, despairing, as well she might, of making a life with such a husband, was pursued by a famous international charmer and finally succumbed to his attentions. George was delighted, seeing in this situation the possibility of a divorce. He consulted his lawyer, who warned him of the financial consequences, which, under California law, are heavily loaded against a husband. George devised a crafty scheme to insure himself against this risk.

Late at night on Christmas Eve, wearing dirty blue jeans, a sweatshirt and a beard, accompanied by two detectives and carrying a brick that he had carefully gift-wrapped, he stealthily crossed the lawn of Zsa Zsa's house and placed a ladder against the wall. Followed by the detectives, he then climbed to the balcony outside her window. All was silent and dark inside when abruptly he shattered the glass with the brick, opened the catch, stepped into the room, turned on the light and, holding out his gift package, said "Merry Christmas, my dear!" Zsa Zsa's companion sprang up and rushed into the bathroom—too late, for the detectives had got their incriminating photos before the sleepers could realize what was happening.

Zsa Zsa behaved with perfect aplomb. Smiling and putting on a lacy dressing gown, she said, "George darling! How lovely to see you! You are just in time to get your Christmas present, which is under the tree. Let's go down and have a glass of champagne and I will give it to you." She led the way downstairs, laughing gaily, gave George his present, gift-wrapped, and poured champagne for the detectives, who were enchanted with her. Indeed a good time seems to have been had by all on that festive occasion, except by the gentleman in the bathroom.

When the impending divorce was announced, their statements to the press were brief and typical. "George is a wonderful man and I shall always love him," said Zsa Zsa. "I have been cast aside like a squeezed lemon," said George.

Divorce may seem a natural and indeed sensible solution to problems which confront a young married couple today, but in my youth it was considered a cataclysm, attended more often than not by scandal and gossip, especially if a third party was involved. I can remember a time when a certain kind of men's footwear, white with leather trimmings, was known as "Co-Respondent Shoes" because when his photo appeared in the newspapers, usually over the caption "The Co-Respondent on the Front at Deauville," he seemed always to be wearing them. He often acquired a dashing reputation, but the woman who became the divorcée somehow lost class, whatever the circumstances. There is no doubt that divorce is still a traumatic experience for sensitive people, and not least for their friends whose allegiance is sorely and unnecessarily tried. In this case, feeling as we did so close to both George and Zsa Zsa, my wife and I were determined not to let their problems affect our friendship. We invited Zsa Zsa and her new admirer to dinner and were saddened to see him drink heavily and seem rather quarrelsome with her. Some time later, I mentioned this to George who was delighted.

"You see! Even a Dominican worm will turn!" he said.

3

I now had to admit to a change in my friend. Riding on a tide of unaccustomed self-confidence, he became talkative, and even didactic; he would raise an admonitory finger and preach the lessons which he thought he had learned on the psychiatrist's couch. To be happy, he would tell us, one has only to make an effort of will; unhappiness is wrong thinking; what is required at such times is simply to change one's life situation, to "take arms against a sea of troubles and, by opposing, end them." If misery hems you in like a wall, he said, have courage, pick up a brick, whether gift-wrapped or not, and throw it, whereupon the wall will shatter like glass and you will step into a different life.

Having got himself out of his ridiculous marriage, he now proposed to get out of the ridiculous acting profession, and at the same time get out of paying ridiculous taxes—two activities he despised. He planned to achieve these goals by becoming a business tycoon. He had discovered that it was perfectly legal for an established business to charge off all money spent on research and development—R and D, as it is known to accountants—and he decided to go into the business of financing inventions, which he might develop to the point at which they were marketable and then sell for a capital gain.

He was in touch with an Italian engineer who had invented a process for making records which would be lighter, tougher and in every way better than anything on the market; he also found a fellow who had a process for three-dimensional photography. Taking these two into partnership, he formed a company, Husan Ltd., of which he was the Managing Director because he provided the basic finance. They rented a small factory, hired workers and, as activity increased, sold stock to friends.

He was fascinated by the Italian, who soon assured him that the records were "dominating the market west of the Rockies," and George proudly quoted this to us all. The other fellow was a different type, a taciturn, uncommunicative genius whom George rarely saw, because he claimed to be hard at work inventing a complicated machine for analyzing aircraft fuel, for which, George told us, the big aviation companies were bidding hotly. George himself confined his activities to designing a beautiful office, equipped with deep-pile carpet, modern furniture, intricate lighting and intercom systems, and an enormous semicircular desk. On the door were the words MR. SANDERS, *Managing Director*. An attractive secretary sat outside but had little to do, because George only visited the office from time to time, as his croquet permitted, when he signed checks, pressed buttons and showed friends around. He was a tycoon at last, and we were all very impressed.

When I was playing *My Fair Lady* in Los Angeles, he pointed out to me that I was receiving a very large salary but paying most of it out in taxes at the end of the year. Why not, he suggested, take advantage of R and D by investing in his Husan company, thus assuring myself of a profit in later and leaner years? I don't know whether I was impressed by his air of confident assurance, by his desk with its rows of shining push buttons, or by his attractive secretary who mixed us drinks at the special bar in the corner of the room; but anyway, I wrote out a check for a small investment. The secretary made out a receipt, which George signed, we had another drink and I became a stockholder of Husan Ltd.

About a year later, my accountant complained that we had received no annual statement from the company and asked me to inquire about it. I was in Chicago, still in *My Fair Lady*, so I wrote to George but got no reply. I then wrote to the Husan company. Still no answer. I waited a few weeks until I returned to California and then I went over to the factory. It seemed to be deserted. Piles of records lay around, and several heaps of faded photographs which did not seem to have come out successfully. The furniture and even the carpet were gone from George's office, and so was the secretary, though his name was still on the door. A caretaker appeared who knew nothing, but he said he had instructions to refer all inquiries to George's lawyer, whose name and address he gave me.

Round I went at once, to be told that the business had gone bust. According to his lawyer, George's co-directors had rifled the till. He showed me stacks of bills for the purchase of expensive cars, the hire of aircraft, rent of houses and lavish entertainment in the best restaurants, all charged to the Husan company. Having exhausted the company's assets, the culprits had then sold their inventions to some other sucker.

Where was the Managing Director in all this, I asked, and how was it possible for such things to happen without his knowledge? The lawyer became defensive. Let's face it, he said. George's position was really that of an honorary director, a sort of figurehead, who could not be expected to know about the operation of a factory. He had lost all his money and was deserving of sympathy. I said I would reserve my judgment on that point until I could talk to him, but his phone had been disconnected. The lawyer feigned surprise, and felt sure that I would soon be able to contact him.

After some days of diligent sleuthing, I learned that it was only too true there were no assets: creditors had slapped liens on George's personal bank accounts, the Sheriff had seized his house and his car, and George himself had fled the country and was in Spain, the despised movie business having come to his rescue in the nick of time with the offer of $65,000 for an important part in a picture to be made abroad with Tyrone Power. (As it turned out, poor Tyrone died on the set of a heart attack and the picture had to be recast and made over again; but it is an ill wind that blows nobody any good, and George received his handsome salary twice.)

I attended a few meetings of disconsolate Husan stockholders, who talked hopefully of suing Sanders, but, as he had renounced his American legal residence when he left, this promised to be a difficult matter. I persuaded the stockholders that it was foolish to throw good money after bad and I promised to write to my friend, asking him at least to let us have a statement of the company's affairs, so that we could, if necessary, charge off our losses on our tax returns.

Several months passed with no reply and then one night the phone rang and I was asked to stand by for a call from Japan. Who on earth could be calling me from Japan? I wondered.

It was George, there to make a picture, and he sounded indignant. "I have had your letter," he said, "and I'll give you your money!"

I explained it was not a question of that. I had made my small investment, I said, with the full knowledge that it was a gamble, and was prepared to accept the loss, but I did feel that the poor stockholders were entitled to a statement, or at least some explanation which would satisfy the Internal Revenue Service. After all, I said, he was the Managing Director!

"What can I do?" he bellowed. "I am out of the country! I know nothing about it! It is up to *you* to see the lawyers and get all the information and then tell *me!*"

Our conversation closed on this quarrelsome note.

A chill descended on our friendship after the "Husan Ltd. affair," but I continued to hear about George from others. It was reported that he was still determined to get out of the ridiculous acting profession, and indeed he remained so till the end of his life, despite the fact that it doggedly supported him throughout. He had decided that the only way to accomplish this goal was to change his life situation by marrying a rich woman. There was a widow in San Francisco, another in London and several divorcées in various parts of Europe who might be expected to be well heeled. His name was linked with each in rapid succession, but he was no diplomat and evidently found it hard to convince them that he loved them for themselves alone.

We heard a hilarious story from a very delightful lady in New York who said that he paid her great attention for a few weeks and she found him charming. One day, as they were strolling past Cartier's on Fifth Avenue, the thought came to her that she would give him a little present, as he was leaving the next evening for Europe. In they went and looked at various trinkets. George's eye was caught by a gold fountain pen that, she said, cost considerably more than she had in mind, but she has a generous nature and he was insistent, so she bought it for him.

He then casually mentioned that he was having difficulty about his hotel room for that night and asked if she could put him up in her apartment. This too was rather more than she had in mind at that moment, but no doubt she was intrigued—and anyway, it was so arranged. She is a wonderful cook and she did her best that evening, including a bottle of his favorite Bordeaux wine, after which, without a word, he retired to her room and went to bed, falling instantly asleep. An hour or so later, she decided the only thing to do was to join him. He continued to sleep, and in the course of time she slept too, awaking in the middle of the night to find the light on and George attentively looking at his gold fountain pen.

"Oh, I'm glad you're awake," he said, "because I want to ask you something."

Now it comes, she thought. Now she would understand what was troubling him.

"Of course, dear," she said. "What is it?"

"Do you think," he said slowly, "that I ought to empty the ink from this pen before I get on the plane tomorrow?"

It was some moments before she could answer, and then she replied "I don't know, George, but if you like I could ask the man at Cartier's in the morning."

"Ah! Good idea!" he said, and he put out the light, rolled over and went to sleep again.

When she brought his coffee to him in bed, he was in a cheerful mood, because he had thought of a new way to beat the tax men, which he was describing to her with delight when she interrupted him.

"Please don't mention taxes," she begged. "I am in the most awful spot. I owe fifty thousand dollars in back taxes, and there is just no way I can pay it!"

George gave her a startled look, got up and dressed, packed his bag and left. She said there was no doubt her unfortunate remark had put an end to their relationship.

4

The so-called Golden Age of Hollywood may be said to have extended over three decades, the 20s, 30s and 40s. About 1933, I had reluctantly realized that the theater world of London and New York could not provide sufficient employment for an actor like myself, whereas the coming of sound to the screen had produced a strong demand in the motion picture world for experienced actors from the stage. I was flooded with offers from the Studios. I had therefore, and with much trepidation, given up my flat in London, packed my few New York belongings and moved to Beverly Hills. In doing so, I had entered a new and rather frightening world composed of high-pressure business people and artists of all nationalities whose lives centered around motion pictures.

For a time I had felt very lost and lonely, but then I discovered a number of British actors, directors and writers whom I had known in London in my youth. Their friendship was a great comfort to me, for I found Ronald Colman, Benita Hume, the Nigel Bruces, Basil Rathbones, Aubrey Smiths, Cedric Hardwickes, Madeleine Carroll, David Niven, Philip Merivale, Gladys Cooper, Dame May Whitty and others, whose hospitality and companionship, whether at home or on the golf course, enriched my life. I became especially close to Ronald Colman, a modest, intelligent and distinguished gentleman who was one of the few great silent stars to weather the change from silent to talking pictures and who went on to achieve even greater fame. It was a joy to his friends when, after years of apparently resolute bachelor-hood, he married my old friend Benita Hume, and this happy and exemplary marriage was to last for twenty years, until Ronnie died at their home in Santa Barbara in 1958.

Pretty, witty, civilized and intelligent, Benita had been the toast of the London stage in her youth and now settled down as a contented wife and mother, the most charming hostess and loyal friend in Hollywood. She was also one of the most entertaining letter writers to be found in a world from which the art has almost gone, and a letter from her was always an event, as her many loving friends can testify. Throughout my six-month tour with Katharine Cornell and *The Barretts of Wimpole Street* company for the American armed forces in Italy, France, Belgium and Holland in the hard winter of 1944 she wrote to me constantly; and when I married my Eleanor in 1946 and took her out to live in California, the Colmans were the first to entertain us at their beautiful home on Summit Drive in Beverly Hills.

As the years passed, we saw a lot of each other, meeting on Saturday nights with a small group of close friends, either at their house or at ours, and sometimes at our desert ranch house. I say "a small group" because Ronnie was rarely at ease with newcomers, who found him reserved and reticent, but to those who knew him well, as I came to do, he was a very dear and valued friend, despite the fact, I am sure un-suspected by him, that we were several times considered for the same parts, both being free-lance actors without Studio associations and both having the same agent.

It was only a few years ago that Frank Capra, while talking to me about the old Hollywood days, mentioned a small select dinner party given by the famous Hollywood screen-writer Frances Marion at her house, which, he said, was the most embarrassing evening of his life. "Why was that?" I asked, and he looked at me with astonishment.

"Didn't you know the purpose of that dinner?" he asked incredulously.

Nothing unusual, as far as I knew, I replied.

"It was arranged," he said, "so that I might meet you informally and offer you the leading part in *Lost Horizon!* The awful thing was that very afternoon we heard that we could get Ronald Colman, and of course you know that meant a million dollars in the box office—a lot of money in those days! It was too late to cancel the dinner, and I could say nothing to you, but I thought you knew, and I sweated all evening!"

No, I said, this was the first time I had heard of it, twenty years later.

On another occasion I was set, but not yet signed, for the famous part of Sydney Carton in Dickens' *Tale of Two Cities*, to be produced by David Selznick at M.G.M. This was a very great opportunity for me, and when the day came that the Studio called to say that Mr. Selznick would like to have a talk with me I went to his office with the script under my arm in a state of euphoria.

Selznick was, as always in my experience, both charming and direct. He was extremely sorry, he said, but the Studio would have to withdraw the offer made to me. I was of course ideal casting for the part, but they had just heard that they could get Ronald Colman for it, and he knew I would understand that meant a million dollars at the box office, so they had no choice.

There was nothing I could say or do but smile, thank him for his courtesy and wish him luck with the picture, but both he and I knew he had dealt me a crushing blow. Outside his office I stood in the California sunshine stunned with disappointment and misery. Dickens' opening line in *A Tale of Two Cities* is "It was the best of times, it was the worst of times," and in the space of those few minutes I myself had passed from one to the other.

The famous novel had been dramatized many years before into an equally famous play, *The Only Way*, which had been produced by the great English actor-manager Sir John Martin Harvey. Anybody who saw it, as I did in my youth, will never forget his magnificent performance and his final line as he stood on the scaffold before the guillotine, "It is a far, far better thing that I do than I have ever done. It is a far, far better rest that I go to than I have ever known." There was not a dry eye in the house. Harvey played the part all over the world to universal acclaim. At one time my sister Elana was a member of his company, touring England and Canada and playing, among other things, Lucy Manette in *The Only*

Way. Now this jewel, certain to be ranked in the Academy Awards class, had come to me—only to be suddenly withdrawn and given to my best friend, Ronald Colman!

That night, by an extraordinary coincidence, we had arranged to have dinner together at his house, and as we sat drinking at his bar I plucked up the courage to ask him if the rumor was true that he might be going to play Sydney Carton. To my surprise, he seemed doubtful and unenthusiastic. Selznick, he said, was insisting that he shave off his mustache, a thin but famous line which had become his trademark and without which he feared the audience would scarcely recognize him. This may seem a frivolous objection now, but in those days it had a definite validity. In the theater, versatility was admired, but the great stars of the screen were those who projected an image which caught the public fancy and then stayed resolutely with it, no matter what the part. Whether Colman, Gable, Cooper, Bogart or Stewart, they always played themselves, and the public loved them for it.

"Don't you agree I'm right?" asked Ronnie.

I hesitated, for in that moment Satan tempted me. If I advised Ronnie to insist on his mustache, it was possible that Selznick would turn to me and I might play Sydney Carton after all!

"Let's think about it," I replied as I handed him my empty glass. In silence he mixed the Scotch and sodas. My heart seemed to turn over. Could I do this to my friend? He added ice, stirred the drinks, put mine before me and raised his own.

"Good luck old man," he said casually.

"Luck to you, Ron," I managed to reply.

We both drank, and I spoke of other things. I could not bring myself to do it.

In the end, he shaved the mustache, played the part and was fine in it, but he never knew how close he came to losing it. Our friendship was not disturbed.

During the War, the Colmans had headed the Hollywood division of the British War Relief Fund, for which the British Colony in Hollywood worked very hard, traveling all over the country to speak at meetings, contributing and raising very large sums of money, and sending supplies of all kinds to beleaguered Britain. Many wonderful letters came back to us, some of which I kept for years until I asked myself why; and two were very interesting, concerning as they did ambulances for which I had subscribed. One came from the head of the Red Cross in Liverpool, who wrote just after the great German air raid which did horrendous damage to the docks and town. He wrote that fires were burning everywhere next morning and there were many dead and injured who could not be picked up because three of their four ambulances had been hit and the fourth was out of order; but as they stood there in despair, a brand new ambulance drove in for which the driver asked him to sign a receipt. Walking around it, dumbfounded with admiration, they came across a little plaque inside which said it was a gift from Mr. Brian Aherne! The second letter came from a driver in far-off Eritrea, who thought I might be interested to know that he had driven his ambulance for thousands of miles through North Africa, the Middle East and Abyssinia and it was still running fine. He enclosed a photo of himself sitting on the roof.

When America entered the war and the invasion of North Africa took place, I myself went over to entertain the troops, and it was then that Benita Colman began to write to me regularly. Unfortunately I did not keep her delightful letters, and the one that follows now was written at the time of the death of King George VI. It came to me after a visit the Colmans made to New York while I was playing with Alfred Lunt, Lynn Fontanne and Edna Best in Noël Coward's *Quadrille*. They had by then sold their big property in Beverly Hills and moved to a small but charming house which they built on the grounds of the San Ysidro Inn at Santa Barbara, an enchanting hotel of which Ronnie owned the controlling interest.

Monday

Darlings,

How lovely to hear from you, although it is we who should have written first to thank you for a wonderful time and most of all Brian for a wonderful performance. Ron and I were tremendously impressed, thought you struck exactly the right note, so humorous, so flighty and yet so attractive, and so truly in the period—all very different from your *Henry the Fifth* on that T.V. Omnibus programme which sparked Ron into writing the only fan letter I have ever known him to put on paper! Fans of yours, that's what we are, and we only wish you appeared before your adoring public more often.

I must tell you that I have been thinking of you both ever since we left New York in an anguish of embarrassment— although actually the reason, which I shall now tell you, is rather funny. In the rush of leaving, I didn't have time to get some flowers myself, but having seen some of my favorite garnet roses in a shop I sent over a note that in Hollywood would have been enough for about four dozen, and left it contentedly at that. As I was in the Plaza lobby, about to leave, I saw the same roses in their flower shop and the price met my startled gaze. My heart quailed as I realised that what you must have received could have been of a size to be worn with perfect propriety by Brian in his button-hole at the King's funeral! Wasn't it too *awful!* I am very much di-minished by the whole affair.

We had a memorial thing here too. Ronnie read a lesson with all his usual grave beauty, Doug Fairbanks (bien en-tendu) did the other one, a tongue-twister beyond belief but no fluff of disastrous proportions, Cedric did the eulogy and apart from knocking over the microphone—such an unsuit-able prop in a church, dear—did very well. It all took place in the L.A. Cathedral which has all the grace and beauty you might more readily expect in a cement factory. Flashlight photographers popped up from every hassock, and the

Bishop made such a speech that I hear there is a movement afoot to put him up in bottles instead of Nembutal.

We loved reading about your flocking paper-hangers, especially as we have also had the house full of four painters this last week, and I may tell you that *two* of the fellows had *gorgeous* Cadillacs to come to work in! "Any time's overtime" is obviously their theme song.

We haven't done anything about your tenants, whom I am dying to meet and am steadily trying to warm up my fellow about. Of course you know with what reckless enthusiasm he greets the idea of *"filling* the house with strangers!" The Steins asked us to a party the other night and I said to Ronnie "I suppose you don't want to go?" He looked at me with absolutely guileless astonishment and said "Are you *mad?"* I must say it did make me laugh!

There is no great scandal here at the moment. The Wanger thing is in abeyance till May. I saw Joan the other night and of course couldn't resist having a slight "behind my fan" chat with her. She seemed wonderfully tranquil, although a few bubbles of anxiety occasionally bubbled up through that bog of beauty. Apparently Walter is keeping his plans to himself and she does not know which way the cat is going to jump. I hope the whole thing will die on the vine. She *did* tell me she has plenty of stuff on him however, which I imagine would put a spoke in his wheel at least as far as representing himself as the pure and outraged husband is concerned. Horrid fellow.

I must be off and pick up my Juliet. Fondest love to both.

Benita

5

My story is about the life and death of George Sanders, and the reader may wonder why I have introduced the Ronald Colmans at this time and why I present a letter from Benita, but patience will be rewarded, for it will be found that all our lives were destined to be interlocked in the most intimate and unexpected ways over the succeeding years. This letter is only the first of many which, as the pages turn, will throw light upon the history and character of a strange and fascinating man.

Correspondence is not created by contact but by separation where there is desire for contact, and we old friends were all separated for long periods of time by the exigencies of our profession. Ronnie was a dedicated painter who worked in his studio and had no time for writing letters. My wife Eleanor, who writes charmingly, does so only on occasion. Benita and myself and, to a lesser but vital extent, George were the main protagonists of the action, and I count myself lucky to have kept their letters, which came to light in a back room of my house in Santa Monica when I sold it recently after thirty-two years' occupancy. The essential element of separation was at first provided by my absence on the national tour of *My Fair Lady*.

Everyone will agree that when that show opened at the Mark Hellinger Theater on Broadway in 1956, it burst upon the theatrical world like a giant thunderclap. The combination of Bernard Shaw's famous play, Alan Jay Lerner's brilliant book, Frederick Loewe's entrancing music, Moss Hart's incisive direction, Oliver Smith's settings, Cecil Beaton's costumes, and the wonderful performances of Rex Harrison, Julie Andrews, Stanley Holloway, Robert Coote and the whole company produced a show which, by common consent, surpassed even the legendary musicals for which Broadway had so long been famous.

The critics raved; people who rarely went to the theater fought, bribed and conspired to get seats; audiences applauded wildly and came out walking on air, humming the glorious melodies and glowing with pleasure. The story ran that a woman came alone to a matinee with two orchestra tickets in the fifth row, sat in one seat and left the other empty. The people around her became so curious that during the intermission they asked her reason. Some weeks before, she explained, her husband had managed to buy the tickets, but unfortunately, a few days before the performance, he had died. She knew he would have been heartbroken if she missed it. But couldn't she find a friend to enjoy it with her? someone asked. Ah yes, she had tried, but that afternoon they were all at her husband's funeral.

It was with keen anticipation that my wife and I arrived in New York during the second week of the run, and we were lucky enough, thanks to the kindness of Rex Harrison, to get house seats and share in the universal joy: I say universal, because I had met nobody who did not share in it. After the show, we were invited to a company party down in the theater bar, at which we met the wonderful people who had given us so much pleasure.

Amid the general euphoria, I had a long and interesting talk with Moss Hart, an old acquaintance and a great man of the theater, to whom I expressed my admiration of the tremendous performance of Rex Harrison, who rarely left the stage for the three hours the curtain was up, except to change his clothes with lightning rapidity, handling the musical numbers and playing each scene with sharp intelligence, impeccable style, variety of pace and attack. I remarked what a pleasure it must have been to direct such a consummate artist. Moss replied dryly that it had been far from a pleasure in New Haven.

Now New Haven, Connecticut, has long been a date which is anathema to the theatrical profession. Close to New York, and therefore the cheapest town to which a company can be taken for a pre-Broadway tryout, it has a large and well-managed theater and an intelligent audience; it also serves as a convenient break-in point before a Boston opening. Many a show has "bombed in New Haven" and disappeared; some, after frantic rewriting or recasting, have gone on to success in New York. It is universally hated by actors, partly because they are in a state of extreme nervous tension at an opening and partly because the old hotel, which is adjacent to the theater, used to be reputed the worst in the U.S.A. It was there that poor Margaret Sullavan, suffering from nervous exhaustion, lack of sleep and a couple of disastrous dress rehearsals, in a desperate effort to get a few hours rest before opening night, locked her door, took a handful of sleeping pills and died. This may have been a mystery to others, but was perfectly understood by the acting profession.

The day of the New Haven opening of *My Fair Lady* must have been torture for everybody concerned. A dress rehearsal, the first with a full orchestra, started at ten A.M. and went on till five P.M. As usual, everything went wrong—music, scenery, lights, costumes, cues—everything. The show was then considerably longer than the version seen on Broadway; a long ballet and a couple of numbers for Higgins were cut out by the time it reached Philadelphia. Rex, whose experience up till then had been in straight plays, must have been unprepared for the confusion and strain of a big musical, and his role of Professor Higgins is, theatrically speaking, the dynamo of the piece. I can well imagine the nervous and physical strain to which he must have been subjected that day, not to mention the effort of remembering thousands of lines, many of them shouted over the blare of an orchestra at his feet. When the curtain fell at last, he stumbled to his dressing room and sent a message to Moss Hart, asking him to come at once. Moss and producer Herman Levin found him in a state of collapse. It was no use, he gasped. The performance that night must be canceled. He simply could not go through it all again.

Consternation reigned. Lerner and Loewe were sent for. They begged, pleaded, cajoled and stormed at him. The house was completely sold out and cancellation was impossible, because there was no time to inform the audience. The show *must* go on, they told him! Rex, armed with the courage of despair, was adamant. Dragging on some clothes, he pushed through the angry crowd, got to his dismal room next door, and locked himself in, refusing all phone calls.

The local radio station was informed and interrupted its program to put out an announcement that the opening of *My Fair Lady* had been postponed till the following evening, but most of the audience either did not hear it or were already out to dinner, and by seven-thirty the theater was already filling up. At eight o'clock, when the curtain was due to rise, Rex was still locked in his hotel room, and they had to plead with him through the clósed door. Finally he was persuaded to come out, and the curtain rose to a restive house some time after nine, not falling till around one A.M. The show received a great ovation, but it was obvious that it needed drastic cutting, and this it received in those hectic out-of-town weeks. By the time they reached the Hellinger Theater, everybody connected with it was utterly exhausted, but the opening was a triumph, and the rest is history. However, as Moss related this story to me, I had the impression that he would never forgive Rex for New Haven. Subsequently, I was to have the impression that the antipathy was mutual.

It was at this party that my old friend Robert Coote, whose inimitable performance of Colonel Pickering contributed so much to the show, remarked that Higgins would be a great part for me. The idea had not occurred to me, because I was still under the spell of Harrison's performance and could not then imagine anybody else doing it; besides, I told him, I had never been in a musical show. Coote laughed. "Neither has Rex," he said. For a few moments I thought about it, but then put it out of my mind. I was never a type to go chasing after parts, always assuming that if any producer wanted me he would ask me, and furthermore it was obvious that Rex would be playing it for the next couple of years at least.

My wife and I were en route to Europe, and a few days later we sailed to England, where we picked up a new car and drove to Spain. After a happy visit with the Richard Aldriches in Madrid, we joined Ambassador and Mrs. John Lodge at the Feria, or spring fair, in Seville, and there we first heard the record of *My Fair Lady*, which had just come out in New York and had been sent to them as a gift. At a cocktail party for American residents and visitors, the Ambassador played it, and we were the objects of universal envy because we had actually seen the show. As we drove on through Spain, Morocco, Mallorca, France, Switzerland and Bavaria, we sang "Wouldn't It Be Loverly," "A Little Bit of Luck," "The Rain in Spain," "I Could Have Danced All Night," "On the Street Where You Live," "Just You Wait, 'Enry 'Iggins," and "Get Me to the Church on Time," off-key and with only a smattering of the words.

By mid-August we were in Bad Gastein, a rather gloomy cure place in the Austrian mountains filled with aged and arthritic visitors, and there one day I received a letter from Herman Levin which startled me. It had been decided, he said, to send out early in the following year a National Company of *My Fair Lady*, which would open in Rochester, New York, and play St. Louis and Kansas City for a couple of weeks each before runs in Los Angeles and San Francisco, after which it would play other big cities across the country. They would like to know if I would be interested in the role of Higgins. I replied that I expected to be back in New York in three weeks, when I would come to see him, and asked if he could wait that long for a decision. He kindly cabled agreement.

There now ensued much discussion with my wife and others. I think I knew in my heart that I would make every effort to do it, but Higgins, as I well realized, is indeed the dynamo of the show and needs tremendous vitality: three hours a performance means twenty-four hours a week under conditions of extreme strain, nervous, physical and vocal, and despite the baths of Bad Gastein, I think I felt older at that time than I do now.

I would have to leave my comfortable, organized life in California and return to the traditional life of the traveling actor, which is spent in strange cities, second-rate hotel rooms, dirty trains and buses, and broken-down old theaters, which in some cases had been unused for years. I had also to consider my wife, who could not be abandoned at home in California and would have to share all the hardships of "the road" without the occupation that I would have. It is hard to ask a woman to sit in a dreary hotel room every evening—and all afternoon and evening on Wednesdays and Saturdays—waiting for an exhausted husband to come home after midnight. On the other hand, a theatrical producer also has great responsibilities, and I felt pretty certain that Mr. Levin would want me to sign a very long contract.

All these things weighed upon my mind from the day I got his letter until the day, some three weeks later, when I met Herman Levin at his New York office. I found him both amiable and alert. Coming straight to the point, he asked me if I thought I could play Professor Higgins. Yes, I replied, I had no doubt about it, but I did not know if I could handle the musical numbers. I asked if he could give me a pianist and two weeks in which to study them, after which I would like to give them all an audition on the stage of the Hellinger Theater. He agreed at once; that, he said, was exactly what they would all like, but they had hesitated to ask me. I started work the next morning.

It was very hot and humid that September in New York, and we had no air-conditioning, but my pianist was relief conductor for the show and knew it thoroughly. Together we worked hard on two difficult numbers: "I'm an Ordinary Man" and "Accustomed to Her Face." I learned to sing them with the music and then, on the first day of the second week, he told me that, while retaining the melodies in my mind, I must now speak the lines to the music with no suggestion of singing. At first I found this difficult, but he assured me that Harrison had found the same problem, and Lerner and Loewe were absolutely insistent that this was what they wanted.

Later, they themselves explained to me that they had worked for a long time on the making of a musical version of Bernard Shaw's *Pygmalion*, but somehow they had never been satisfied with the result, so they had put it on the shelf and worked on other things. A couple of years went by before it suddenly occurred to Lerner that the mistake lay in their conception of Higgins, whom they had naturally thought of as a tenor who sang his numbers, just as Eliza does; they had even written a duet for the two of them in which Eliza protests she is too nervous to go to the ball and Higgins entices her, singing "Come, come to the ball!" All this was wrong, he told Loewe. Higgins is, after all, a professor of the English language. Speech, clear and correct English speech, is his fetish. "Why can't the English teach their children how to *speak*?" he cries.

The springboard of the play is his acceptance of Colonel Pickering's bet that he cannot in six months teach Eliza to lose her cockney accent and transform her into a lady by teaching her to *speak* correctly. In scene after scene, he teaches her, cajoling her, bullying her, storming at her until finally he succeeds, only to find that she has touched his heart and he cannot lose her. "Damn! Damn! Damn!" he cries, and then to himself he says,

> I've grown accustomed to her face.
> She almost makes the day begin.
> Her smiles, her frowns, her ups, her downs
> Are second nature to me now,
> Like breathing out and breathing in. . . .
>
> I'm very grateful she's a woman, and so easy to forget,
> Rather like a habit one can always break—and yet—
> I've grown accustomed to the trace
> Of—something in the air—
> Accustomed to her . . . face.

If he sings this, ending perhaps on the traditional high note, it is a nice romantic song and no more. If, however, he speaks the lines angrily, resentfully, while the violins softly whisper Loewe's enchanting melody, we seem to hear the still, small voice of his heart speaking and, for those few moments, magic is created.

Once this realization came to Lerner and Loewe, they told me, the whole show fell into place. All their reservations and doubts vanished. Everything worked.

"Therefore," they said to me, "don't sing, Brian! Whatever you do, *don't sing!*"

Frederick Loewe, as the composer, might have been expected to resist this idea, but he was especially adamant about it and would burst into Harrison's dressing room—and later into mine—to expostulate if we so much as indicated the tune in a single line. "Also," he would add in his charming Viennese way, "they might recognize some of it, and I don't want that!"

Incidentally, if any doubt is felt of the wisdom of this decision, one has only to listen to the original recording of *My Fair Lady* and then to the one which is marketed today —made, I believe, in England about three years later. In the original, Harrison speaks clearly and sharply throughout, but in the later record he lapses into song all too often; his Higgins suffers in consequence. He also does it in the movie, and I don't think that Frederick Loewe could have been around during production!

At that time, I did not know that when the National Company was being planned, the management had combed the American theater to find the right people for the four leading parts, and then, to the anger of the Actors Equity Association, they had gone to London, where they auditioned every available English actor. They were more or less agreed upon the casting of Eliza, Pickering and Doolittle, but still had not found a Higgins. It was Levin's assistant who, while leafing through a casting directory, had come across my name, and so I had received the letter in Bad Gastein. Now, some weeks later, they were just as nervous and uncertain as I was when we all met at the Hellinger Theater.

I gathered myself together. "Well, let's have a bash at it!" I said. They retired to orchestra seats—in London we would say "the stalls"—while my faithful pianist and I climbed onto the empty stage, lit by one naked rehearsal light and furnished with a battered old upright piano. We ran through the numbers without difficulty, and when I came to the end they were already on their feet. We all felt a wave of relief. I was to play Higgins—we all knew it was settled—but the great question in all our minds was for how long? How many years? Nobody ventured to bring it up at that moment, but I looked at Mr. Levin and thought that a difficult interview lay ahead. Perhaps, I thought, I should be represented by some clever fellow in the negotiation of such an important contract.

The head of the theatrical department of the Morris agency at that time was a nice fellow, and I strolled uptown to have a chat with him. The opening and closing lines of a chat with one's agent are roughly the same, and this one was no exception.

"It's so good to see you Brian," he said as I entered. "Tell me, what can I do for you?"

The obvious answer to this is "Find me a job," but that didn't fit the situation this time, so I told him instead that the motion picture industry seemed to have come to a stop, at least as far as I was concerned, and I was contemplating a return to the stage. I asked if he knew of any impending production that might have a suitable part for me. He replied that unfortunately he did not, but of course he would keep his eyes open. I moved to the window and looked down on Broadway; far below, I could see the lights of the Hellinger Theater marquee announcing the matinee of *My Fair Lady*, and, with my eyes fixed upon them, I asked if there were not perhaps some big musical going out on the road for which I might be suitable. I had always wanted to be in a musical, I said, and would not mind going out of town.

He thought a bit and then shook his head. "I'm afraid I don't know of anything, Brian," he said, "but we'll certainly bear it in mind. Thanks for coming in. Always such a pleasure to see you. Be sure to let me know if there is anything I can do for you."

Nothing worth 10 percent of my gross, I decided, and it was quite possible that he had another client up for the part. So, after mutual expressions of esteem, I left him and walked across town to see Arnold Weissberger, good friend and lawyer to many of us in the theater. He negotiated me a splendid contract, and even persuaded Mr. Levin to sign me for one year certain, with the understanding that I would stay with the show for as long as I felt able to do so.

The following evening I saw the show for the second time, and afterward my old friend Rex Harrison came out to supper with me. In a secluded corner of the Oak Room at the Plaza, he spoke like the seasoned pro that he is. He wanted

47

me to realize, he said, that the part of Higgins was—to use his own word—a man-eater! The first essential would be to take great care of my health, to rest whenever possible, to take a walk each day to get fresh air in my lungs, but no strenuous exercise, for I would get plenty of that on the stage. I must cut out smoking altogether, because the strain on the voice was so great. Rex is thin and wiry, and younger than myself, so I listened to this advice with close attention. What about the musical numbers? I asked him. Were they not a nervous strain for straight actors like ourselves?

"My dear fellow," he replied, "I give you my word: when that bloody orchestra starts, my heart stops!"

What about the "Hymn to Him" (better known as "Why Can't a Woman Be More Like a Man")? I asked. It is one of the most brilliant numbers in the show, but the rapid lyrics, many of them deceptively similar, were giving me trouble. He instantly agreed. Sometimes, he said, he would misplace a couple of words and then, realizing what he had done, would blow the whole thing.

"Good God!" I exclaimed in horror. "Don't tell me that! What do you do?"

He would stand there, he said. The orchestra would go racing on and he would just stand there until something came back to him. However, he had recently devised a clever scheme: he had the lyrics, in large type, pasted on the back of the set just outside the center door, and now if he blew a line he would simply walk upstage, glance around the corner and carry on from there.

"Doesn't the audience notice?" I asked him.

"How the hell do I know?" said Rex. "They don't seem to."

At this point, I had lost interest in my supper and was beginning to lose interest in the idea of playing Higgins, but Rex was determined to help me and to point out every snag. It was very important, he told me, that I should not become confused by the rapid changes of scene, which were accomplished by means of blackouts and a huge revolving stage, there being only one intermission. The batteries of lights were many times more powerful than those used in straight plays, and when, on cue, they all went out, I would find myself in pitch darkness. The stage would start to revolve, the music would rise to cover the noise of the change, and I would bump blindly into singers and dancers moving to their places for the next scene. This was a moment, he warned me, when panic could set in, and it would be advisable to have someone experienced standing by ready to seize my arm and propel me rapidly to the entrance, right, left or center, through which I must dash as the lights came up again. I should also practice certain changes of costume while on the run and in darkness.

What about the awesome galaxy of talent with which I would be working? I asked—Moss Hart, Alan Jay Lerner, Frederick Loewe and all their satellites. To whom could I turn for sympathy and support in rough moments? Upon whose artistic judgment should I rely? Normally, of course, an actor turns to his director, and often leans upon him, but what I wanted to know was whether I could lean upon brilliant, mercurial and probably egotistical Moss Hart. Rex thoughtfully downed his whisky, looked at the ceiling and then said, "Alan Jay Lerner." The man was a genius, he said, no doubt of that.

At one point in rehearsal it had become evident that a scene was needed which would bridge the gap between the quarrel after the return from the ball and Higgins' discovery that Eliza is living in his mother's house. They had all met after work for discussion over a drink in Rex's hotel suite. One idea was that we should see Eliza packing and running away from the house to music, another that attention should be concentrated on Higgins' reaction to the discovery that she has gone. It is a vital point in the story, which suddenly stops being a Shavian intellectual exercise and confronts us with man and woman in the age-old conflict. How is it to be resolved? When Eliza tears off the rented diamond necklace and throws it at Higgins and he stalks out in a fury, the audience will be agog to know what happens next. Moss Hart, always deeply interested in psychology, was analyzing the behavior of both characters when he made some remark about its being a pity that men and women seemed incapable of understanding one another.

Lerner sat up and put down his drink. "Wait a minute!"

he said. "I think I've got it! I'm going to work now. See you tomorrow!" And with that, he left. Next morning he came to rehearsal with the corridor scene, complete with the famous "Why Can't a Woman Be More Like a Man?"

After some further discussion of technical details, we parted, and I can never be sufficiently grateful to Rex for his interest and his genuine eagerness to help me in the task that lay ahead of me. One result of our talk was that I decided it would be foolish to commit myself for any longer period than I felt able to do my best in the part, nor would I attempt to imitate Rex but would try to give my own performance. I signed the contract a week later and returned to California to study and to fulfill some television engagements. From my house in Santa Monica, I was able to walk along the deserted beach in the mornings, declaiming Higgins' words to the waves and the sea gulls flying overhead, so that when the time came to return to New York for rehearsals I felt reasonably secure.

Only three weeks were allotted to the whole production. In the mornings we had costume and wig fittings, collected our make-up and so on. At noon we all met in the small auditorium on the roof of the New Amsterdam Theater and rehearsed the play until a break for dinner at five. At seven we returned to rehearse the songs, dances and ballets until ten or later.

About a week before we started, Moss Hart was struck by agonizing pain in the abdomen, which was diagnosed as a kidney stone. He was rushed to the hospital, and there was doubt that he would be able to direct us. A few days later the English members of the company arrived, and I was awakened next morning by a gleeful telephone call from Robert Coote, asking if I had seen the newspapers. My Eliza, an excellent young actress named Anne Rogers, had been taken to see *My Fair Lady*, and on the way out of the theater reporters, alerted by the management no doubt, had asked her how she enjoyed it. Her widely quoted reply was "Well, it's a pretty good show, but I don't think it's all it's cracked up to be—but then, you see, I'm from Cheshire!"

"From Nutsville, Cheshire, evidently," chortled Coote and added that this should be a fine stimulant to business all across the country. He also reported that one of the English actors had had to be supported off the plane, as he was blind drunk.

"Better be prepared for a strong aroma of whisky on stage, old man!" said Coote, and alas, he was right.

I arrived early at the first rehearsal, and to my surprise, for I had not expected him to be there, Moss Hart was sitting alone on a bench at the back of the stage, looking very white and shaky. I could see at once that he was a sick man, and in a highly nervous state, as well he might be.

"Brian!" he cried. "I'm glad we are alone for a moment. Come here and sit down. I must talk to you!" As I sat, he grasped my wrist and glared at me with burning eyes. "Now listen!" he said. "Three weeks is not enough for us, and the pressure on me is going to be very great. I warn you, you must not oppose me! I know myself, and if you do oppose me I know what will happen. I shall have no time to fight you. I shall just ignore you. I shall say to myself, All right, let the son of a bitch go to hell! You will suffer in consequence. So I'm warning you now—*don't oppose me!*"

I was astounded by this vehement onslaught. My years in Hollywood had taught me that the director was always un-questioned king of the set, and furthermore I stood in awe of Moss, whose tremendous reputation, trenchant mind and outspoken manner rather frightened me. I admired him very much, and what I was hoping for, and indeed expecting from him, was the kind of sympathetic help and encouragement which had been given to me by a director such as Guthrie McClintic, through five Broadway productions. I knew that Moss had just come from hospital, where he had had an agonizing experience, and the thought occurred to me that this must be some sort of sick-room fancy. I was still staring at him in amazement when the company began to file on stage.

"Moss," I said weakly, "I would never dream of such a thing. I admire you far too much. I'm sure we'll get along fine, but we haven't read a line yet. Let's have a bash at it, shall we?"

The stage manager interrupted. Introductions were made, we sat on the usual hard chairs and fumbled for forgotten pencils. Scripts were distributed, and the first reading of the play began. Charles Victor, a fine old English actor, read Doolittle superbly. Comparisons, as Mrs. Malaprop says, are odorous, but he was at least as good as Stanley Holloway, and indeed he never failed to bring the house down wherever we played. When we came to the end, there was a nervous silence while Moss conferred in undertones with the stage manager. Looking at the small managerial group which faced us in the first row of the orchestra, I caught the eye of Frederick Loewe, who gave me a little wink and a slow appreciative nod of the head. I was greatly comforted.

It occurred to me later, and I think I was right, that Moss was confusing me with Rex Harrison, about whom he seemed to have an obsession, for he always expected me to speak and move exactly like Rex. I soon gave up the idea that I would be allowed to create my own performance, and indeed our rehearsal time was too short to permit it, so that we played for some weeks before I could shake off the necessity to imitate him.

Moss worked with feverish intensity and great expertise, but in the second week he collapsed once more and had to return to hospital for some days, during which we were able to enjoy a period of calm under the quiet, friendly direction of Alan Jay Lerner. Moss came back, however, in time to pull us into shape before we left for Rochester, where we opened the tour.

A technical crew, whom we never saw, traveled ahead of us to each town to rig the revolving stage and instruct the local stagehands in the operation of lights and scene changes. Our own heads of departments traveled with us and put in many hours of hard work before each opening in a new town. Taken together, we were a small army of actors, stage managers, dancers, singers, understudies, musicians and conductor, with wives, husbands and pets—dogs, cats, birds in cages, and even goldfish—so that it was necessary to have a special train to carry us; and I am afraid the reputation of traveling theatricals cannot be too good with the railroads, because our "special" usually consisted of the most battered and ancient rolling stock they could find: two baggage cars, three sleepers, a chair car which had a stand-up sandwich counter, and an old locomotive which hauled us slowly along, with many stops on sidings to let the faster traffic through.

Rochester provided us with an enormous auditorium, the forerunner of many similar caverns, which returned gross weekly receipts unheard of at that time. All went reasonably well on that opening night, and a charming supper party was given for the company by the local residents afterward. Moss had many notes for everybody at rehearsal next day, after which he flew back to New York, together with Lerner, Loewe, Levin, Cecil Beaton, Oliver Smith and their satellites. We were left in charge of our manager, Joe Grossman, who had his work cut out, handling all our problems as well as those of the front of the house. Show folk, however, are friendly folk, which is good, because they are thrown very much together and, because of their working habits and hours, rarely have the chance to meet anybody in the towns which they play.

It was to be fourteen months before Moss Hart, in response to pleading letters from myself, came at last and rather unwillingly to Chicago, by which time I felt the show needed him badly, as all shows need their director from time to time. George Abbott once dropped in to see one of his shows running on Broadway and put a notice on the board saying: THERE WILL BE A REHEARSAL AT 11 A.M. TOMORROW TO TAKE OUT THE IMPROVEMENTS. The constant repetition of a performance, eight times a week, can lead the most conscientious actors into changes of pace, emphasis and timing, which may or may not be improvements, and this only a director can determine from the front of the house. In my belief, a director should want to see his show at least every month.

Our company of *My Fair Lady* was very conscientious, and I think that, apart from one unhappy incident, the performance kept up remarkably. As I later told Mr. Levin, little Anne Rogers was a gold brick to the show, singing beautifully and apparently tirelessly, never losing her concentration or enthusiasm, resourceful in any emergency onstage, and always thoroughly professional. In London she had played the lead in *The Boy Friend* for four years without missing a performance, and Julie Andrews had been her under-study. Our management had wanted her to play Eliza in the Broadway production but she could not leave her show, so they took Julie instead, and I think this had been a heart-break for Anne. However, she was to play in our National Company for two years and eventually played Eliza with Rex Harrison at Drury Lane in London, continuing after he left the cast until she had been with it for three years, a total of nine years in only two shows, which surely must be a record for any actress! No wonder that the specter of unemploy-ment, which haunts all members of our profession, never seemed quite real to her.

After Rochester, we moved to Detroit and on to Kansas City before opening the City Light Opera season in Los An-geles, where, as usual, we sold out clean for the ten-week booking. Next came another terrific eight weeks in the huge San Francisco Opera House, where I lost my voice one night and my understudy had to replace me. This had never hap-pened to me before. When I got in the following night, Charles Victor poked his head in my dressing-room door, looking like a wise old bird. "Take it easy!" he said. "Save your voice!"

"It's such a gigantic house, Charlie," I replied. "I want them to hear."

"You want your money more, don't you? It's no play, no pay, you know!" he said and disappeared.

On we traveled, to Denver, Des Moines, St. Louis, Dallas, Indianapolis and Chicago, where the show settled down for a two-year run before it went on again around the country, spending two more years as a bus-and-truck company in the smaller towns. Always we were greeted by massed and cheering audiences. Always we read glowing notices in the local press.

Lerner and Loewe both came to San Francisco and Indi-anapolis, traveling on with us to Chicago for the opening there. After the show, they gave a grand supper dance for the company, at which Lerner took me to one side. He ex-pressed his gratitude and admiration to me. "You have made the part your own, Brian," he said, and he then wanted to know how long I would stay with it. What did I want to do?

He would help me in any way I wished. I hesitated. Should I not discuss these matters with Mr. Levin? I asked him. He answered that he and Loewe had full control of the artistic side of the production. In that case, I said, when my contractual year was up, I would be happy to sign for another if I could follow Harrison into New York, where I had an apartment and my wife could be close to her family. I also told him that it was my dream to play Higgins in London, either to follow Rex or, if he didn't want to do it, to open there. After nearly thirty years away, it would be a triumph for me to return in *My Fair Lady*. Very well, he said, he would bear these things in mind and do what he could for me.

About six months later Herman Levin arrived to see me. My contract would soon be coming to an end, he said. For how much longer would I sign?

"How much longer do you want?" I asked.

He laughed. "Five years," he said.

I tried to explain about my conversation with Lerner. He listened impassively, and then he asked, "With whom did you sign your contract?"

I was taken aback, and of course I had to admit that I signed it with him.

"Very well," he said, "then you discuss it with me, not with Mr. Lerner!"

I did not want to tell him, and indeed did not do so till some years later, that my wife was at that time suffering from a severe nervous breakdown, which made life in Chicago very difficult for me. Instead, I told him that I would play four additional months upon completion of my contract, but if he could put me in New York I would make it a full year. He seemed surprised and displeased by my attitude, and gave no indication that he had discussed the matter with Lerner.

We had some further negotiations during the following weeks, and I almost wished that I had allowed the Morris agency to handle things for me. He wrote that on Rex's departure they had moved the understudy into the part at the Hellinger, and it was now impossible to change the arrangement.

Suddenly I myself fell ill of a mysterious malady which

had no unusual symptoms except that I could not get up and walk across the room! I was out of the cast for three dreadful weeks, with poor Joe Grossman calling every evening to know if I could go on. An eminent doctor, warmly recommended by Noël Coward and the Lunts, diagnosed mononucleosis and filled me with pills, with no result. A specialist was called in who affirmed that I had nothing of the kind. A psychiatrist was recommended but could not see me for a month. My poor wife continued to be in very bad shape. In desperation I called Lynn Fontanne in New York, and in her decisive way she told me to go at once to their lovely house at Genesee Depot, Wisconsin. I was supported into a car and driven up there. It was a glorious spring, and I lay out in the garden, surrounded by peace and beauty, until in a few days I miraculously recovered. I believe now that I was suffering from nothing more than acute nervous exhaustion. Returning to the show, I played till the end of June, when we both went home to Santa Monica, sixteen months after the opening in Rochester.

I did not play Higgins in New York, nor was I asked to play it in London, and at the time I was very distressed. I suspect that somewhere I got lost in the crosscurrents of a managerial dispute, but still *My Fair Lady* was the greatest experience of my theatrical career, and, coming as it did late in my life, it remains a glowing memory for which I shall always be grateful.

6

It was while I was in the middle of my breakdown in Chicago that I suddenly received an astonishing phone call from George, whom I had not seen for a long time. He had heard that I was in trouble, and as he had planned to fly from New York to Los Angeles the next day he proposed to stop in Chicago and come into town to lunch with me, to cheer me up! I had been feeling so lonely and in such despair that I was deeply touched by this unexpected gesture, coming from such a man and involving as it did so much trouble and inconvenience for him.

However, no contact with George was without its surprises. The gaiety and warmth of his arrival evaporated after his second vodka, when he launched into a diatribe against the acting profession, which he said he considered unworthy of an intelligent man. Now I have always had some sympathy for this point of view, and indeed I was in later years to write a book about it, but at that moment I was starring in the greatest part of my career in what I considered the best musical ever written. I was out of the show, the business had dropped, and there was doubt if I could get back on stage again. I was in a very nervous condition, I resented his attack and a heated argument developed, in the midst of which he had to leave his unfinished lunch and rush off to catch his plane to L.A.

I continued the discussion in a letter in which I asked if he realized how much he owed to the profession he affected to despise, and how little he gave to it; it was well known, I said, that he never bothered to learn his lines before coming on the set, fraying everybody's temper and wasting hours of costly time with cool indifference, although his striking personality had kept him always in demand and had provided him with a comfortable fortune. I was in no state to be provoked, and his visit had been intended to cheer me up! It did not succeed! Here is his reply, which illustrates my comments upon his original views.

December 31st 1957

Dear Brian,

I was very happy to receive your angry letter, and I am glad I shook you up a bit. Ask yourself this question: if money (greed); loyalty to theatrical tradition (pernicious exhibitionism); rigid conformity to social convention (masochism), are incompatible with personal happiness—which should be sacrificed?

You talk about the theatre as if it had some cosmic significance. As a matter of fact it is pathetically sublunary; a drab and dusty monument to man's inability to find within himself the resources of his own entertainment. It is usually rather fittingly housed in a dirty old building, whose crumbling walls occasionally resound with perfunctory applause, invariably interpreted by the actor as praise. A sad place, draughty and smelly when empty, hot and sick when full.

I wonder which is the sickest, the audience which seeks to escape its miseries by being transported into a land of make-believe, or the actor who is nurtured in his struggle for personal aggrandisement by the sickness of the audience.

I think perhaps it is the actor, strutting and orating away his youth and his health, alienated from reality, disingenuous in his relationships, a muddle-headed peacock forever chasing after the rainbow of his pathetic narcissism.

My love and best wishes for a happy New Year.

George

While I hardly think that it was such beliefs that brought on the backache which got him out of the *South Pacific* engagement, this letter of course delighted me. I had it framed, and it hangs in my study in New York City, where it engrosses my theatrical friends to this day.

Letters from Benita Colman were of a very different character. Those immediately following, although undated as was her regrettable custom, were all written during my tour of *My Fair Lady*, at which time we were concerned about Ronnie's health. He had complained about feeling ill for some time, but the doctors seemed unable to diagnose the cause, and I think that Benita, who always enjoyed excellent health herself, had almost come to believe that his mysterious problem was psychological, possibly connected in some way with his retirement from the screen.

SAN YSIDRO RANCH
MONTECITO
CALIF

Darlings,

It is just as if you were touring the Milky Way, you have become so remote! Still, I have your "routing" so I can at least track down what constellation you are working. Brian, you will have to pull a Gunther and write a book about the American Hinterland. I was going to suggest calling it *Inside My Fair Lady* but that looks rather coarse!

We are just about to go down to Beverly Hills for a couple of days at the chest clinic there to see if they can find anything new, right or wrong, with Ron, who remains rather miserable, poor dear, it's a bore for him. He consoles himself with painting some very high-class pictures and we are all exhorting him to have an exhibition because June-the-former-Lady-Inverclyde, as the press reverently refers to her, has one down in the town which I feel would do credit perhaps to the Pavement Artists Union, but Santa B needs some *talent* to elevate the local standards.

Well, the clinic turned up nothing particularly new except that it won't be nearly as bad as Ronnie feels at the moment. He can really do anything as long as there is no strenuous exercise involved. These chest things may affect the heart if you aren't careful. He can travel anywhere by plane but shouldn't carry luggage, run for trains or climb mountains, so I tell him there's no sense bewailing being unable to swim the Channel when he's not going to anyway. But he's pretty good today.

We had the Boyers to dinner down in Beverly. He's about to start *The Buccaneer*, which Ronnie had also been asked to do, and it's a real bugger! Charles is already regretting it madly, which made Ronnie laugh and feel very set-up that he had turned it down.

The Harrisons have sold their house with all the usual Harrison farce attached. The buyer was pronounced a person of immense importance and secrecy, whose name could not be divulged. When he came to view the house everyone— but *everyone* was to be out. After some argument, one maid might open the door. Should Mr & Mrs H. come home and see a strange car, they would please drive on. Faint with curiosity, we discussed the possibilities: then the secretary cheated and took a peep and gave her considered opinion that it was King Carol of Roumania and Mme Lupescu! Of course we were all *enchanted*. What a delicious dénouement! Lilli taxed the house agents, who were quite convulsed with secrecy, and we all became certain it was them. By this time we had all been to parties where everyone said the Lupescus had bought it. Even the *Reporter* said so, and added they were *staying* with the Harrisons! At this point, Lilli and Rex came home and found a Washington representative sitting with a grim face in their home and demanding a quick explanation of what they were doing harboring foreign royalty to the great embarrassment of the Government! Well, the house was bought and the signatures perforce appeared and there, bold as brass, was written—William Powell!!!

It's all quieted down now, but it was quite a panic while it lasted. That about brings us up to date.

Lots of love from all to all.

Benita

I used to wonder how Benita Hume, after the gaiety of her youth spent in London or at country house parties, and aboard palatial yachts at Cowes or on the French Riviera, could stand the years of monolithic boredom in Montecito, where the Colmans never mixed with the rich socialites who comprise the local population, but I never heard her complain. However, it is possible that Ronnie's continued illness may have turned her thoughts to the possibility of life in Europe, where the total change of surroundings might be good for them both, and where Juliet might receive a more rounded education than Santa Barbara could offer. Benita's best friend, Mrs. Nigel Bruce—"Bunnie" to us all—was now a widow and had returned to live in England; she was prevailed upon to find a country house in Berkshire which the Colmans could rent for the summer. Unfortunately, it turned out to be directly below the take-off patterns for the London airport, and furthermore, having spent so many years in California, the Colmans had no friends in England, barring a few theatricals, so altogether their holiday was not a success.

STONEHILL HOUSE
ABINGDON
BERKS

Darlings

I don't know what it is, but there's something about other people's desks and these foul ball-points with which one travels which makes the whole idea of sitting down and writing insupportable, but your letter has persuaded me to bear the burden!

First of all—and your shrewd eye will no doubt discern my attitude as being on the defensive—the weather, as I predicted, has been one long heat wave! The children picknicked (picniced?) every day in the surrounding meadows under those lovely trees we are always looking for in California. The house is not *bad*, pretty and Queen Anne, but there are no proper reading lamps, too many flies, and a chatty old cook of the meat, two veg and castle pudding type, absolutely sans élégance to say the least! We also have a maid who gets £1 a day and is doing her best, such as it is. The clutch on my beautiful Jaguar started to slip violently as we *left* the *Savoy* which resulted in an hour's delay at the work-shop, and is now slipping *again* so they are fetching it today leaving me with a stinky Humber Hawk for a week.

Ronnie developed a stiff neck as we arrived in Plymouth which he still has and this morning for good measure has a slight temperature and general aches and pains and is in bed! He is something less than intoxicated by the whole project so far!! The children—Juliet and Geraldine Chaplin —left for Switzerland yesterday and I think we are going too in 10 days to have a look at schools and possible pieds-à-terre for ourselves. Tuesday we go up to Stratford to stay with the Oliviers and see *Macbeth* and *Twelfth Night* which I hope will be fun. Lil Palmer came down last Sunday and we all went over to Notley Abbey for a cocktail. We sat in the garden—heavenly! Marlene was there, and I must say look-ing awful, which was sad. The English countryside is still lovely as ever and there is a local pub called "The Rose Re-vived" which even Ronnie likes, but I believe he is chroni-cally depressed here, claims the roads are unbearably over-crowded—they really aren't you know—and can't face driving on the left etc. Of course there is no doubt the Jaguar is like driving a *truck* after a Cadillac! And then the goddam clutch did nothing to raise his opinion of local transport.

Lil Palmer is alternating breakdowns with Rex and every-thing sounds very highly coloured, his love affair waning as hers begins to bloom and she playing a fine dramatic role of whether to stay with Rex or run with Latin lover. I don't know how it will work out but she is still an enchanting girl. I love her, so hope for the best. [Lili ran with her handsome Argentine, Carlos Thompson, a talented writer and fascinat-ing man. They married and lived happily ever after.—B.A.]

Bunnie is in rollicking form and George Cukor is so enthu-siastic about her I'm sure she will wind up taking Ida Kov-erman's place at M.G.M.

I think it *awful* about your *Apple Cart*—*Swan* mix-up and would have thought *The Swan* a much better bet as you can surely do *Apple* later on when you find a good cast, which is madly important in that particular piece. It really could be ruined by having the wrong woman in the second act. I can't get Ron to go to London, damnit, so probably won't get any information on the girl you mention. Your party made me die! Isn't it pure hell? And imagine the barefaced treachery of Merle, calling to say you would surely *"understand"* her preferring another invitation! Really there is no end to people's effrontery!

Which reminds me, the Fairbanks gave the most *colossal* blow-out for us—well, I don't really know how much it was "for us," but in any case I should think over 100 people for cocktails and supper. In the garden, bloody cold dear, everyone looked *too* awful in the daylight and Eileen Plunkett's make-up made her look like a Dufy. Ronnie's neck got *very* bad (!) and he insisted on leaving about 10 p.m., thereby missing Princess Margaret—I'm sure to Douglas' great chagrin! However Prince Bernhardt was there and some little Dutch Princesses to keep everyone hopping up and down, and the Mountbattens and Danny Kaye and the whole boiling blue book. To tell the truth, I had a fine time, but then my snobbery though intermittent is unconcealed and it is no effort at all for me to be fascinated by a bore as long as he is couched in a castle!

We had a very highly spiced version of the George Sanders –Zsa Zsa histoire from Lilli which I must say left us limp with laughter! There is something irresistible about a man who cultivates caddishness to such Homeric proportions!

Oh DO come over for a bit! I really think you might be tolerably comfortable here. I don't think we shall stay till the end of September.

Come on!   Love darlings.

Benita

STONEHILL HOUSE
ABINGDON
BERKS

Sunday

I do love your letters. They make me laugh so much. I would like to have one every day!

This is the situation. The thing is that I am sure Ronnie will never enjoy anything here, he doesn't like the house, doesn't want to go to Dunrobin Castle for a visit, or to Leeds Castle to see Olive Bailey, doesn't want to go to the theatres or anywhere, and feels so ill it seems pointless to battle with obviously insuperable odds, whereas I think if I can get him to Switzerland—which I hear is beautiful at this time—I think he might buck up and become a yodelling type. So come and join us! We'll look around there and then get an *enormous* map and go over the Brenner Pass into the Austrian Tyrol, then we could meet the Carl Esmonds who are in Munich and perhaps Gottfried Reinhardt who I hear is in Salzburg. Does that sound like fun? I am putting Juliet and Chrissy on an earlier boat and we will fly back.

DO come! Fresh woods and pastures new! Don't forget, on Aug 9th we shall be at the Beau Rivage Hotel. Ouchy. Lausanne.

I now hear that Sanders actually has proposed marriage to Sylvia's sister, Vera, and has been turned down, so she has more sense than is immediately apparent perhaps. Ron thought it an unforgivable indiscretion that she told anyone, but I said that since it is possibly, or probably, the only respectable suggestion George ever made to her it was only fair that she should give him the credit due!

If you fly to Geneva, we will take the Jag over and have a luggage rack put on top. The four of us would be quite comfortable.

Lots of love

Benita

Of course nothing would have pleased us more than to have joined our dear friends in Europe, especially as I had at last finished my engagement in *My Fair Lady* and would have welcomed the holiday, but I had become embroiled in a situation which Benita refers to as my *"Apple Cart* mix-up."

This was brought about by a man in New York who aspired to become a producer on Broadway by reviving Bernard Shaw's play of that name, which had been done recently and successfully in London with Noël Coward in the lead. Somewhere he had found an "angel" who was prepared to put up the necessary capital, and he offered this part to me when I was leaving Chicago. After some negotiation I signed a contract, and as the play would not go into rehearsal for three months, I looked forward to a rest in California and time to study the part of King Magnus, which is of enormous length.

As the weeks passed, I began to have fears about the experience of the producer, who consulted me at every point and seemed to rely upon me to do the casting for him. I tried unsuccessfully to persuade Greer Garson to play Orinthia and corresponded with London about a star for it, meanwhile cramming the lines into my head and making plans to lease our house once more in our absence.

One day, coming out of the dentist's office in Beverly Hills, I met Mrs. Charles Vidor, who asked if I was working, and I told her of my hopes and struggles with *The Apple Cart*. She then told me that her husband, who had directed me in three successful films, including my all-time favorite, *Lady in Question*, was about to do *The Swan* at M.G.M. with Grace Kelly, Alec Guinness and Louis Jourdan. They were hunting for an actor to play the delightful part of Miss Kelly's uncle, an amusing priest, and upon seeing me it suddenly occurred to her that I would be ideal for it. I said I thought so too, but had to explain that I was tied up with King Magnus.

A few days later I received a telegram from my producer saying that he had lost his angel and asking if I would care to invest in the production—and this less than a month before we were due to go into rehearsal! My first action was to phone Charles Vidor and tell him I might be available, my second to demand my release from my theatrical contract, but this the would-be producer flatly refused to give me. Meanwhile M.G.M. declared they must have an immediate decision.

It seemed I was about to fall between two stools, and in desperation I called the local representative of the Actors Equity Association, who could not bring himself even to admit the possibility of a member unilaterally breaking a signed Equity contract.

At this moment the Colmans called from England to plead

with us to join them on a trip to Switzerland. Hearing of my dilemma, they both reacted like the pros they were:

"Defy the bastard!" they cried. "With a starting date in three weeks he has no money, no director and no cast! Why, he will break the contract himself! Sign with Metro and to hell with him."

I did just that and have never regretted it, for all eventually turned out well. The following year Maurice Evans took over *The Apple Cart* and did it with Signe Hasso. Meanwhile I played in the film of *The Swan* and enjoyed it, forming a delightful and enduring friendship with Her Serene Highness Princess Grace—the perfect title for her—which, more than twenty years later, brought my wife and myself an invitation to Monaco for the marriage of her daughter, the Princess Caroline.

HOTEL BEAU RIVAGE
LAUSANNE—OUCHY
SUISSE

Darlings,

Well! You see we have got ourselves over here, and I must tell you immediately that I think all that stuff about "The Swiss are so dull, aren't they, and does one want to *live* there" is a lot of poppycock. It seems to me the most civilised and enchanting country I have ever visited. It isn't just the scenery, in fact it isn't the scenery at all, one mountain and all the boring clichés to which it gives rise being in my estimation very much like another. It's the whole place that's delightful. The villages are much prettier than in France and haven't that ill-natured Proust-ian air about them. On the contrary, they are clean and jolly, and so filled with growing flowers and hanging flowers and potted flowers that one expects the whole population to be given place cards by Ouida Rathbone at any moment! The smallest shops are gay and rather chic—not at all like Abingdon dear, where the 'addocks languish under a rich quilt of bluebottles and the greengrocers exhibit a few despondent peaches sitting in rather sordid straw.

Now they are haymaking, always the prettiest harvest but here quite breathtaking with hay carts and horses and children and sunbonnets—and the *scent!* How lovely! Then to top it off there are the orchards, which are past belief! Pears and plums and apple trees knee deep in grass and Queen Anne's Lace standing in a sort of stupor of summer ripeness, loaded with rose-coloured fruit of such beaming beauty that you find yourself smiling fatuously back at them as you go by!

Now the Chaplins (make no mistake at all) are living like kings! The populace worships him, the house is *lovely*, the "parc" is *lovely*, the society elegant and the luncheon superb —also the wine—and their *flowers* make Santa B. *nothing* in comparison. They are extremely warm and friendly—which rather took us back a little to tell the truth!—and we are having great fun with them. By the way, Kay Kendall arrives tomorrow with Rex!!! We are trying madly, and at the moment alas unsuccessfully, to find a house to buy. We *must* live here. It is under two hours to Rome, London and Paris, it is divinely beautiful in summer and winter, and there is virtually *NO TAX!!* And very low death duties. It isn't cheap, but if one doesn't have to pay everything to the Government that isn't so bad. I am just mad about it.

Ron still has the bends and isn't feeling or looking at all well. I don't know what to do about it but we are planning to move up to an hotel in the mountains with walks and country: these lakeside ones are of course rather urban and we are staying partly to get the laundry done and partly to use the real estate agent in Lausanne. Moreover we have the Prince of Wales Suite here, in which one could comfortably give a ball for 200 people but not so comfortably give a breakfast for two! Tomorrow we are going to the famous Fête des Vignerons in Vevey which is apparently terrific and only takes place every twenty five years. I hope the weather holds up as the arena is open and it was *pouring* this morning and we have yet to see the Dents du Midi mountains for which Ronnie searches angrily every day whilst explaining to me where they are and indignantly declaring they were always in the *clearest* blue sky when he was here before! I just saw Tilly Losch. Do you remember her? [Yes, of course.—B.A.]

I asked her in for a drink but now I've the doctor coming in for Ron so it's rather complicated. He is calling himself Camille Colman now!

I'm so glad *The Swan* came off and hope you survive the much touted charms of Miss Kelly, whose acting I regard as a real atomic age thundering bore, but anyhow I make no doubt you will steal the show handily with your beard and cassock and side-saddle and all.

I think I told you that Larry is *superb* both in *Macbeth* and *Twelfth Night*, which latter he plays with a rather adenoidal refined cockney which is *heaven*. Viv is, I hate to say, a disappointment but looks beautiful and is well and flourishing. And that's the lot.

All our love

Benita

This lyrical description of Switzerland is no more than that remarkable little country deserves, and this remarkable lady had the taste, intelligence and grace to enjoy it. She saw it at its best, however, and there have been changes in the intervening years which are not for the better, but the flowers are still there, the fruit blossoms, the geraniums and petunias dripping from window boxes, and the wild white narcissus sweeping over the mountain slopes in June. The Fête des Vignerons, a glorious festival of music, dancing, costume and color, which four times in each century packs the market square of Vevey with an audience of 16,000 people daily for two weeks, came to us magnificently this year. The ancient farmhouses, the Hotel Beau Rivage and some Chaplins are still there, and Benita was to see it all again and even to live there as she wished, although under surprising and very different circumstances.

Since she wrote that letter, there has been an influx of Italian and Spanish workers, widespread building of square high-rise apartments, and miles of high-speed autoroutes have been constructed, all in the name of progress and the advancement of the masses. The tax situation is, alas, no longer as she describes, although the Swiss system of government is so different from those of either the U.K. or the U.S. that it is hard to compare them.

Many people are surprised to learn that the existence of Switzerland as a unified country is comparatively recent in history. It was Napoleon who took the first step by occupying the Cantons of Geneva, Vaud and Valais to ensure the safe passage and communications of his army into Italy over the St. Bernard Pass. He actually made an attempt to include the Canton de Bern but was repulsed by the warlike Bernese. This is why French is the official language of those Cantons today while Bern speaks mostly German.

Some years after the Congress of Vienna, the surrounding powers—France, Bavaria and Austria—recognizing the need of a buffer between their mutual frontiers, agreed to unify the mountain Cantons into a confederation—the Confédération Helvétique—and to guarantee its neutrality. About 1836 there was even a revolt of some Cantons that wished to secede, but it was put down.

The Confederation imposes only one tax upon the incomes of all Swiss citizens and residents. It is for the national defense, and there are few objections to it. The individual Cantons, being still largely autonomous, make their own laws about local matters. The law of the Canton de Vaud, in which we live, is based upon the French Code Napoleon, which is different in many respects from our English law. One is taxed, for example, on one's *train de vie*, which means that the local officials take a long hard look at one's house, cars, servants (if any, but they have almost vanished) and one's obvious expenditures generally, and then they think of a number, double it and send a demand biannually. Benita says of that time, "It is not cheap," but she would be horrified at the present phenomenal rise of the Swiss franc, which has cut the incomes of foreign residents to one third and driven many of them from the country.

In due course, the Colmans returned to Santa Barbara and we drove up to stay with them. Not having seen Ronnie for quite a long time, I was very distressed by his appearance, but he took my arm and said laughingly, "Oh, don't look like that, chum! I'm not going to die, you know!" The doctors had at last discovered that he was suffering from emphysema. Cortisone was tried and gave some relief, but within the year he developed bronchitis, was rushed to the hospital and died after a few days there. Coming out of a television studio in New York, I saw the headline in an evening paper and it struck me a crushing blow. We called at once. Poor Benita could not speak to us, but our beloved mutual friend Mrs. Nigel Bruce was with her and told us what happened. Of course we wrote, and here is her answer:

B.H.C.

Thank you darling Elly and Brian for your call and letter. I cannot tell you what this is like, a nightmare, an amputation or a wildly untrue story that Ronnie isn't in the world any more.

Bunnie is here and is my tower of strength. Everybody has been so wonderfully kind. I can't write, darlings. "Our revels now are ended."

All my love

Benita

7

Ronald Colman's death was indeed a grievous blow to all who loved him personally or admired him professionally, all over the world; and our hearts went out to Benita. Within a few weeks, she sold the Santa Barbara property, shipped the entire contents to England and, taking her little daughter, Juliet, she joined her sister Billie Milburne, who was just divorced, in buying a beautiful old house, Weeks Farm at Egerton in the County of Kent. That autumn, we visited them there, and one afternoon as we all sat around a blazing log fire, enjoying an English tea, Benita suddenly said to me, "Brian, you are my oldest and dearest friend, and I want to ask you something."

She paused. I waited. Then she took a deep breath and said "What would you think if I were to marry George Sanders?"

I stared at her in amazement and for a moment could hardly believe my ears. Ronnie, as we all knew, had not approved of Sanders, who was rarely invited to the house, and Ronnie had only died a few weeks before! Indeed we had come over to comfort his widow! I gulped, and then to play for time I asked, "Where is George?"

"He's in Spain, on that picture with Ty Power. He has been telephoning and writing to me every day. He is absolutely *insistent*. And d'you know—I'm half inclined to do it!"

Of course it instantly occurred to me that George assumed Benita to be now a rich woman, and I couldn't help laughing as I exclaimed, "Oh, darling! He's a *dreadful* man!"

"But you are his best friend!" she said in astonishment.

Yes, I admitted, and I might even be his only friend after Stuart Hall, but that was because the unusual quality of his mind interested and amused me. I explained that, in his odd way, Sanders had been a good friend to me and I liked him, but I didn't expect others to do so, and I really didn't think, since she asked me, that he was the kind of man to make any woman happy.

She became very silent after this and did not refer to George again, but about a month later, when we were back in California, we read in the paper that she had married him at the British Embassy in Madrid! After we got over the shock, we cabled and wrote our good wishes, but Benita did not reply, and indeed it was to be months before I heard from her again, and this made me very unhappy, for I loved my friend.

George, on the other hand, was quite unperturbed, as he always was about personal matters, and did not resent in the least my calling him a dreadful man; after all, I had done so for years. "Oh, George," I would say to him in a jocular manner, "you really are a dreadful man!" And he would always take it with a chuckle. As far as he was concerned, the tragedy of Ty Power's death was most convenient and profitable for him, because the picture closed down for several months, enabling him to fly with Benita to Japan and make another, after which he returned to Spain to pick up $65,000 all over again. He wrote to me from there.

GRAN HOTEL

ZARAGOZA

Dear Brian,

The Comparmento of Valdespartera where we are shooting all the battle scenes is only 15 minutes by car from the hotel in Zaragoza where I have an elegant suite. We do one camera set-up in the morning and then break for lunch which is served in the Officers Mess by obsequious waiters. It consists of four courses, with wine and liqueurs after coffee. The food is of a quality only equalled by the best restaurants of the world. After lunch we drive back to the set in our Mercedes-Benzes and then we have a short siesta in our very cleverly designed German-built caravans, each with its built-in lavatory and wash-basin. We do about two camera set-ups in the afternoon and then quit for the day.

We have about three thousand extras—all soldiers who have been trained for the battle scenes since last June. They are paid $1.00 (One dollar) per day to risk their lives riding the chariots, having spears thrown at them and getting trampled underfoot by the horses. Not a day goes by without an accident and the ambulance is kept busy all day long going back and forth to the hospital with the casualties.

Yesterday one of the soldiers went right under my own chariot, he could not see us coming because of the dust and he was part of a group that was running obliquely across our path. The horses caught him square on and trampled him underfoot and he passed beneath us to disappear quivering in the billowing dust that we were raising behind us. A Spanish officer yelled to him to get up and keep running so as not to spoil the shot. He staggered to his feet, ran a few paces and then dropped in his tracks and passed out. The ambulance took him away. It is possible that, if he recovers, the officers will be lenient with him but generally speaking when this happens the officers beat them with their whips until they get up again.

There is of course no doubt whatever that this is the proper way to treat extras.

When I tell you that this location is a bit rough I am referring to the actual battle scenes, in which unfortunately I have to take part. I am a mass of cuts and bruises from riding in my bloody chariot! My sword is made of rubber, my shield of fibre glass, my breastplate of papier-mâché and I have cunningly concealed bits of sponge rubber everywhere in the chariot, and yet by the end of each day I am almost a stretcher case. How those fellows did it for real in the old days I'll never know.

Well, anyway, so much for the picture. We shall be winding up here in a few days time and moving to Madrid. To-night we are giving a concert at the Air Base. Mrs Crawford (wife of an actor) will sing, accompanied by myself at the piano, our distinguished director King Vidor will play Spanish guitar and I am playing again with a three piece jazz combo. If all goes well, I may allow myself to be persuaded to sing "Because" as a very special request number. I know how *that* would please you!

With regard to my situation in California, I have been making some drastic changes. I have given up the house and fired Albert. All my stuff is being shipped to England. I gave Albert my Ford convertible and my piano as parting presents. Albert by now must be a very rich man. He has been borrowing and stealing money from me consistently for many years and I felt that these things would just about top óff his situation nicely.

A deal has been made for Husan where it is now on a royalty basis only and has no overhead and no future operations in the factory. Husan will receive a minimum royalty of $750 a month based on 5% of the gross of Robert Shaw Fulton. [How's that again? —B.A.] This means that as soon as present debts are liquidated, this income will be distributed as dividends to interest holders and to the partners. So it looks as though we are going to get something back on the investment after all. It was a thoroughly worthwhile experience tho' from now on I shall go it alone. I'm not going to fool around with partners. I have only one partner—Benita.

Love and a big kiss to Eleanor.

George

I continued to fret about Benita's silence, and when one of George's postcards finished by saying "Benita still pouting," I wrote her a groveling letter of apology, begging her forgiveness and promising *never* to call him a dreadful man again. George referred to this in his next card, saying, "Don't worry about Benita. Women are excitable and not to be taken seriously. I am sure that, secretly, she strongly suspects that I am a shit!"

Eventually she wrote.

Dearest Ahernes,

What a lovely lovely cutting! I daresay one of the most fragrant blossoms ever picked from the unfragrant gardens of the press! And one is left with absorbing speculations as to how far the lady contributed to the rape, still expecting it to be regarded as one. To climb a 64 ft ladder doesn't seem to introduce quite the right element of chase and reluctance which one normally associates with this kind of hanky panky: in fact I think Mr Pettit should really bring a counter-suit claiming that *he* was the assaulted party!

I am going to London next week to have my horrid hand operation and to see Juliet, and Debbie Power, whom I think a duck and very funny, is going with me. This will mean a long Sanders-separation which I shall hate, although if I am on my own—I shall be staying with Sylvia actually—there is nowhere I would rather be than London. Being here, with George working every day, I find a thundering bore—worth it, I admit, but a thundering bore just the same. I still don't understand why you said so ominously "He is a dreadful man!" I don't think he is dreadful at all—impossible yes, but not dreadful! I can only say that he is the kind of man who makes it a joy to wake up in the morning and find he is there. I haven't laughed so much since I was a little girl. I can't tell you how good his "memoirs" are becoming, he really writes astonishingly well, in fact I am beginning to think being astonishing is his most monotonous quality!

We have a whole new theory bubbling on the hob which is to use a Swiss house for our sober and business side of life and a pink palazzo in the Canary Islands for a sea-sun and hilarity house. We are going to have a quick look around there at the end of the picture, if they don't get held up or late or anything. We think one probably needs sun after a bit and that is the cheapest, nearest, most beautiful and most unexploited place—we'll keep you posted.

I'll bet there's plenty of going on about "us"! I wonder

what the Menjous had to say! Oh well, nothing like stirring up people a bit.

Lots of love to you both

Benita

p.s. We think—and the "we" is emotional and not editorial —that you should take a deep breath, re-arrange your lives and come back to live in Europe, within whistling distance of us. Hollywood is, and always has been for all of us, a professional base in which you have to live in terms of a competitive professional situation which is tiresome and gives one a false set of values, besides being unbearably monotonous and limited to things which don't add a jot or bloody tittle—whatever a tittle may be—to one's happiness. Fresh woods! Fresh woods! Come on, you don't want to loll about there! We are loaded with wild plans but are actually going to Switzerland for a house early next year. Merry Christmas & all that.

B

I was glad to get this letter. I had had my lesson, and she did not refer to my unfortunate remark again. Others did not get off so lightly. The two closest friends of the Ronald Colmans in Santa Barbara had for many years been a couple who, upon hearing the rumor that she might marry George within a few months of Ronnie's death, wrote to her expressing their apprehension: they were unprepared for the blast which greeted them!

WEEKS FARM
EGERTON
KENT

Dear ———

All that has happened so far is that George Sanders, under the most tedious pressure from the press, said that we were to be married in six months' time. I concurred, thus stopping endless gossip and speculation which was neither agreeable nor reputable. I take it you are not so naive as to regard any quotes you may have read as to be in any way related to what was actually said. . . .

The fact is that George (who has been in Spain incidentally while I have been in Switzerland and here) has been the kindest and most gentle man who brought me out of the depths of despair, made me laugh and helped me to start living again. He is also intent upon marrying me, which is not usually considered a very unruly inclination. . . .

I think of love as delight and benevolence and compassion, and the only blessing that makes this almost insupportable life bearable. I do not have to prove to anyone NOW that I loved Ronnie. We proved it to each other, and I suppose everyone else, until death did indeed us part. All our love and life together lies now inviolate, in a pocket of the past. It was full of joy and it is over.

Happily all my friends here, and I have very many, including the Oliviers, the Fairbanks, the Chaplins, are uniformly delighted for me. I daresay the English having been so closely allied to sudden death during the War have a more practical and compassionate view, rather than a parochial one, to the facts of life and to feel no urgent necessity to be ruled by the philosophy of Mmes Parsons and Hopper.

Before I finish, I tell you again how immeasurably I appreciated your most practical kindness in May. I do not know where I would have turned without it. . . . Perhaps you are both at your best when my back is against the wall. I see at the end of your letter you say, "If there is anything we can do, please do not hesitate to let us know." Well, I suppose having been such an old friend I must hesitate in front of such a tempting invitation, but I have an *almost* overpowering inclination to tell you.

Sadly, and clearly with no love, for I do not want to see you again.

Benita

Back in California, pressed by the Husan Ltd. stockholders, and thinking that Benita's absence in London might provide a good opportunity to contact George again on this matter, I now wrote to him, mentioning in the course of my letter that I would like some elucidation of his comments, which were, to say the least, obscure! As will be seen, he answers in typical fashion but gives me no word for the poor stockholders, who were indeed never to see a penny of their money—nor any statement, nor any expression of regret. As far as George was concerned, they didn't exist, despite his fleeting reference to "interest holders" in his previous letter. He seems oblivious to the fact that, had it not been for my intervention, the stockholders would have sued and the consequences for him, as Managing Director, could have been very serious indeed.

CASTELLANA HILTON
MADRID

26th Nov 1958

Dear Brian,

Thank you for your letter of the 18th. Regarding your question as to my reaction to the prospect of an additional stay in Spain, I can only tell you that it makes no difference to me. I have reached that happy state of being indifferent to my surroundings. I have liberated myself at long last from morbid concern regarding the terrestrial co-ordinates of my geographical location. This used to be one of my biggest ambivalences. I have successfully resolved it. I live in the mind, which is the only place to look for happiness.

The trips which you suggest I should make, to Segovia, Toledo etc; I did all those things years ago. They bore the shit out of me. I employ my time staring into space at the hotel or staring into space at the studio and am perfectly happy. On my days off I get up at about eleven o'clock, write my book until one-thirty, then walk all the way to the Ritz Hotel where I have a leisurely lunch preceded by many cocktails. I then walk all the way back to the Hilton where I sleep a siesta. I have become a young Sir Charles Mendl.

I think that once you and Eleanor have got your problems sorted out you may very easily decide to settle down in Europe where you can live comfortably on the income from your capital and not worry so much about work. In America there is so much pressure about *work, work, work*, that it gets into your bones without your realising it. It is a most unhealthy atmosphere. Work is very bad for you if it is too frequently engaged in.

If you were to lease a fisherman's cottage on the Costa Brava or a place in Portugal which is very cheap to live in, and flew or drove to London three or four times a year to do a T.V. show, and also did the occasional part *on a tax-free basis naturally* in some American motion picture production either in Italy or Spain where most of the production is going to be concentrated, you would have a *saner, happier* life. You would have no financial worries and could be very picky and choosy about your parts. Since you would be working tax-free and all your living expenses would be covered by your income from your capital investments, you could afford to cut your price and be swamped with offers from which you would select the acting plums, the gems. Also you would be living *near us!!* which is important for both of us and would add to the fun.

Love

George

He makes three erroneous assumptions in this letter:

1. That the future of motion pictures lay at that time in Spain and Italy, when in fact production collapsed in both countries within a year, leaving no possibility of employment of American or British actors in either.

2. That it is a simple matter to receive salary earned abroad tax-free. It may be in some cases, by setting up holding companies in such faraway places as Curacao, Liberia, Liechtenstein or the Isle of Man, but the tax gatherers will be baying like a pack of hounds at your heels and sooner or

later will bring you down, with penalties. George followed this will-o'-the-wisp of tax freedom for many years, but it only led him on to ultimate destruction.

3. He always supposed that I had somehow acquired a large fortune, on the income from which I could live comfortably without working. My father could have warned him against such suppositions. "One can never know about O.P.M. [Other People's Money]," he used to say. The truth was that I had to work to pay my bills and keep going, and jobs were becoming very hard to find for actors, not many of whom could make any provision for their old age. I once explained this to George, who was of course instantly ready with advice. I should go to the French Riviera, he said (unaccompanied naturally by my wife). It was full of rich widows and divorcées who were rolling in money and lonely. "An attractive fellow like you could pick up one in no time!" He nudged me and winked as he added, "A nice wad of money can be very helpful!" I said I didn't think I would be well cast for the part.

Benita wrote to me on her return from London to Madrid.

CASTELLANA HILTON
MADRID

Monday

Brian dear,

You sounded a little sad in your last letter and George and I talk about you and worry about you—when we are able to spare the time from worrying about ourselves!

They are working like maniacs here and all feeling rather ill, which is not surprising with dinner at 10 P.M. and 6 A.M. calls and everyone with tourista (not me, but I can be just as highly strung when I am quite well and not working). We are trying slowly to unravel our tangled skein of affairs, and really just have to go gradually from one knot to the next and hope it all makes sense one day. I am trying to get John de Bendern's house in Morges to rent, the idea being to start the Swiss bit as soon as possible.

To tell the truth, I am in a fine state of confusion, panic and faint-heartedness, but when Sanders staggers in from the Studio I am so overwhelmingly pleased to see him, and he is so cosy and enchanting and generally down my alley that I am comparatively fortified again! This is definitely my ambivalent year!! As I look at the date, I suddenly realise it is also my ambivalent birthday, so there you are, you see! You are not the only one who forgets things, I even forget my own!

We had lunch with Francesca Lodge who spoke affectionately of you. George didn't like her much so he closed up like a clam which made me giggle—he has the most refreshingly ruthless form of behaviour! I also had lunch and a long gossip with Ty Power's wife who spoke very warmly about you both— I think she is a duck. Lots of love to you both darlings and one or other of us will keep you posted. Let us know what goes on with you, for God's sake.

Benita

8

In 1959 and 1960 I was out on tour with Katharine Cornell in the U.S. and Canada, so we did not see them. George's picture ground to an end, and he and Benita set off on a leisurely trip which was to wind up in London, where George ordered his new Rolls-Royce, and so to Weeks Farm. En route, they sent picture postcards of places where they had finally decided to settle: Marrakesh, "the only place this side of the Atlantic where one can be sure of winter sunshine"; Soto Grande, near Gibraltar, "which has an airport providing direct service to London"; the Costa Brava; Biarritz; the French Riviera ("after all, it has everything, including an international airport"); Le Touquet, "the obvious place if one wishes to be near London without putting one's neck into the British tax-gatherer's noose"; the Bahamas, with "plenty of servants and a reasonable tax structure"; and finally, and perhaps inevitably for Benita, Lausanne, Switzerland, where they established themselves.

It seemed that a miracle had occurred for both of them, and they sailed on a cloud of contentment; although George did once remark to me, confidentially, that Benita had not so much money at her disposal as one might have supposed. This did not surprise me, because I certainly had not supposed that my cagey old friend Ronald Colman would leave his money around for any Sanders to pick up, as it were; and indeed we heard that he had carefully locked it in a Trust, with his daughter Juliet as ultimate recipient. There was some talk about breaking this Trust, and a trip to California was made to see what could be done; but it turned out to be unbreakable, which was welcome news to Benita's friends.

All was well, however. George was himself making lots of money, tax-free no doubt, and his new-found happiness seemed to release his energies. Fortune smiled upon him, as she often does upon those who are happy, and he went from one film to another, in London, Rome, Paris, Madrid, Monte Carlo, Beirut, Budapest, Cairo and even Tel-Aviv, flying to New York or Hollywood for lucrative television engagements between pictures. Together they enjoyed every moment, writing hilarious weekly accounts of their adventures while we groaned about the vicissitudes of a transcontinental tour. Our correspondence became a joy to the four of us. Like George, I was writing my memoirs in my leisure time, and we were both published. I never saw George's reviews. Mine were astonishingly good, but neither of us hit the best-seller lists and both were "remaindered" within a few months. Presumably the libraries have them on a back shelf: George's is called *Memoirs of a Professional Cad*, and mine *A Proper Job*. The writing business is even tougher than the theater.

WEEKS FARM
EGERTON
KENT

Wednesday

Darlings

The impenetrable gloom of your mood about the memoirs I thought madly funny! Your memory is obviously working with too sharp a focus. You'll have to fuzz up the facts a bit, with the delicate distortions inherent in wit, irony, sentiment—or to put it candidly, thumping lies! George just came down for tea and your letter immediately set him off writing your book for you, which set me off adding your Birmingham memories— You should be here—we'd have it finished, out, and scandalising the public in no time flat!

The rain it raineth every day and we leave for Paris and

Monte Carlo tomorrow and then back here for a three weeks' stint, and then to Turkey for *another* one which I think sounds interesting—Troy, the mask of Agamemnon and all that sort of thing. I don't know what the picture is and do not like to ask George as I am sure he considers it an indelicate question. At any rate, he never asks himself, so I conceal my vulgar curiosity as best I may.

Lots of love

Benita

WEEKS FARM
EGERTON
KENT

6th Sept. 1959

Dear Brian

I think you will find that if you tell the truth in your autobiography nobody will be interested and you will find it difficult not to be pompous and dull. It doesn't matter if the title of the book is misleading, as long as it's eye-catching and intriguing, and it doesn't matter if its contents are silly if they are entertaining. As a suitable title for your book I suggest,

INDISCRETIONS OF A FORLORN APRICOT

Chapter one.

"Take that you bastard!" said Joan Fontaine, her strong little fist connecting with my chin. Lightning exploded in my brain and I went down for the count of ten. As consciousness returned, my mind drifted back to my boyhood in Birmingham. I thought of the poignance of first love, the unforgettable spring when Birmingham's air, soft, richly thick and grey, and fragrant like an unwashed bedsock, made my heart beat faster. And she came running towards me, my little Beryl, her little fist outstretched and her high, childish voice crying to me, "Take that you bastard!"

My reverie was cut short by the emergence of Louis B.

Mayer from the bathroom. I understood at once that my career was ruined. I had caught the great L.B. in a compromising situation with my wife! It was unforgivable. I knew then that my contract would be dropped and I would be relegated to spending the rest of my life on tour with Katharine Cornell.

End of Chapter one.

That's the kind of thing to give the public.

George

HOTEL DE PARIS
MONTE CARLO

Friday

Darlings,

Well, here we are in glamorous Monte Carlo, all ready to wind up the picture and do a little high-class lounging in the sun. This however is not as easy as we thought, as since we arrived two days ago the whole coast has been pummelled by storms of such unbridled violence that the lights keep going out and it rains hard enough to knock over a bus. They haven't got a shot to date.

We are staying here in a suite of absolutely paralysing grandeur which M.G.M. really couldn't improve on, but the whole joint is taken over by a convention—yes, I suppose it's spread to France now—on Sunday so we may find ourselves in a very awkward position if the weather doesn't break tomorrow.

George became so intoxicated with the idea of you, with your romantic poetical personality and discreet behavior in life, writing a biography of unwavering savagery, sex and violence that I think if you had not been on separate continents you would have been quite carried away by his lunatic inventions on the horrific life of Aherne and the best-selling potentialities of such a project!

Stan Joël has just arrived on his yacht and asked us to go on board for a drink, but I want to tell you that at this point the downpour is such that really the boat would have no trouble floating upside down.

What was that irresponsible plan you had to sell your house? With jet planes circling the globe in about 2½ hours it hardly seems worth moving—not, I admit, that I am particularly enchanted by the shortness of the flight, it's the *fright* which concerns me, and every form of locomotion seems to bring into sharper focus my craven condition. Honestly, the way those buses tear about the Corniche! I think I may go to the Canary Islands and just have a donkey with a rose behind his ear and a little cart!

Lots of love from both

Benita

CHEMIN DE MONTOLIVET 27

LAUSANNE

Sunday

Darlings—

O *damn!* It is awful you aren't coming for Christmas, we *are* disappointed! *Every*one is here and we now refer to ourselves as The Alpine Set. Yes, we see the Van Johnsons a lot —you *know* they'll never transplant, I simply can't believe that will work—and Noël of course, and the Rubinsteins are arriving for a concert shortly and Noël says that Niven is about to show up too. Then Jack Palance and his wife were here the other night—rather odd I thought them—and Rodney Soher yesterday, my God it's getting to be like the Flight out of Egypt, anyhow we feel no end central and gay.

It's not a bit of use, I'm not going to send Sanders back to you, you'll just have to stop being soppy about him—I have cornered the market in that respect. He is lying in bed at this moment and just asked me with great glee to hand him his razor as he has discovered a new *battery* kind which enables him to shave while lying down and reading *Time*.

We go back to England at the end of the month for some horrible picture about Landru, but it will be fun to be at Weeks. Our cottage is about done and we are putting in a pool! "They" say in the papers that we are in for 20 years of hot summers so we thought we might as well be prepared.

You *must* come here you know. We are simply loaded with projects, going to build apartment houses and become all shapes and sizes of tycoons, one day we might even have a house with a guest room! Still and all, I do know there's nothing like giving a cracking performance, having an ovation and topping it off with a modest, incredulous bow! And then we're missing all those lovely T.V. shows which are coming on this fall. I must say that's rather maddening. Larry O. has got the most marvellous notices here for *Disciple*. I wonder if you have seen it yet. Viv opens tonight in London in Noël's *Lulu* thing; apparently they are gradually getting together again—I mean Larry and Viv—after quite a period of storm and strife, so we'll be able to see that when we get back. I'll leave the rest of this for George.

Lots of love always

Dear Brian,

Do buck up and make enough money to be able to give up all those silly activities you seem to find it necessary to engage in, and come and be a bum in Europe. One discovers new advantages every day over here. The actual breakaway is difficult—at least, I found it so and I know you would—but it is something I'll never regret. There is a wonderful sense of being liberated from the American rat-race and of being able to contemplate it from the proper side of the Atlantic which more than compensates for the loss of the good things America has to offer. When you come over next spring we shall be solidly entrenched and we will go into all these things in depth.

Love
George

p.s. Who won the Sam Goldwyn Croquet Cup?

CHEMIN DE MONTOLIVET 27
LAUSANNE

Darlings,

You didn't send your itinerary—what a miserable word that is—in your last lovely letters, for which thank you, so we don't know where you are. I saw Pat Medina in London, we lunched together and she told me you were an absolute knockout Brian in the play, so there you are, knocking the lovelies over like ninepins, a gratifying pursuit if ever there was one!

We are of course outraged there is no theatre for you in New York—not so much that it separates you from your urban triumphs, in which we only enjoy a vicarious pride, as that it separates you from us which of course we take as a personal affront! Well damn! We shall have to save each other for our old age if this keeps up.

I must tell you with a fierce glee that it is *heavenly* here. *Thick* snow, and we go into the mountains to a ridiculous Disneyland of chalets where we slide down the main road on sleds and George makes a dignified if leisurely descent down the slopes on skis 12 inches long, thereby becoming in turns sneered at, closely observed, talked about and finally affectionately regarded as the local eccentric by the aficionados.

We were joined in Verbier by Van Johnson who is currently surviving a crisis with Evie which culminated in a great deal of flying furniture at Gstaad over Christmas. They were here yesterday prior to her returning to the U.S. this week. However, over prolonged tea and drinks they became so dewy-eyed we wound up wondering if they would not stay together after all! Not that anything would be achieved by it I think. They are not in the least happy with each other.

We dined with Noël. His house is lovely and he is as contented as can be. Viv Leigh was there. She looks lovely, weighs about 20 lbs and is quite obsessed with misery, for Larry has apparently left forever. She wept and wept, and I felt very sad and don't know what may happen. I thought, apprehensively, she seemed far too interested in Margaret Sullavan, who had joined the Do-It-Yourself Club in the papers that day. I wish all our friends weren't so highly strung.

George is recuperating from his siege of work and is now in a creative frenzy. He spent the afternoon ecstatically immersed in a lot of incomprehensible machinery designed to fill the joint with music. This resulted in our being plunged in darkness several times and finally a dim voice filtering through from the roof. However he emerged beaming with satisfaction and is currently applying porcelain door knobs which, rather unexpectedly, involved a hacksaw (which removed all the paint over a considerable area) and an electric filing device on which he burned himself and had to be succoured with kind words, praise and poultices. Still, to give credit where due he does the damndest things quite beautifully and I am in a constant state of stunned admiration. Yesterday he drew an enchanting cover for the book, not liking what had been suggested, and I hope they use it for it couldn't be cuter, but who ever knew George could draw before? A formidable fellow, that's what he is!

We might go to Nassau next month to stay with Olive Bailey— Seems like getting a sunburn the hard way though, such a huge trip. Have you ever been there?

I *do* hope you get back at least to England soon, we miss you madly. Why can't you open in London before New York? Maybe we could all be there in the spring and do lots of Weeks-ers with bicycles & primroses & picnics & that class of thing—we have to go back in May to pick up George's Rolls Royce!! That is, if it is ready. All he is getting so far is a series of little notes saying it will not be completed quite as soon as was previously thought—honestly, I don't know how that Island has enough nous to keep its head above water!

We have people for lunch—we also have a chef with a hat 2 yards high!—so I must go and function. Lots of love to you both.

Benita

p.s. Since this, a lovely fat letter from you which George will answer—it made us *long* to see you. For God's sake, tire of your triumphs soon and come back to us!

CHEMIN DE MONTOLIVET 27
LAUSANNE

21st Jan 1960

My dear old horse,

Whenever we get a letter from you it is a joyful and relaxing event. News of its arrival spreads like wildfire. Laughter is heard. Out in the courtyard the children start skipping, jumping and clapping their hands in unrestrained merri-ment. The organ-grinder on the corner seems to turn his handle faster as though suddenly released from the bother-some restrictions of musical tempo. Monks in the monastery of Montchoisi start buggering each other with renewed vigour. Everywhere there is good cheer and good-will. Such occasions are in marked contrast to those which obtain when other letters arrive: then depression and gloom reign supreme, for it only means more work—the time-consuming bore of answering them.

The fact is we are so busy that we never seem to have time for anything. Benita works in the sitting room, I in the library at letters, bills and things like that, or in my attic workshop fixing something for the flat, which never seems to be getting any nearer completion. Our exacting needs are hard to satisfy. We have four servants and a secretary, all of whom, plus ourselves, are dedicated to the task of making our little nest comfortable and workable. I sometimes wonder if we have bitten off more than we can chew, whether we shouldn't have settled for a Volkswagen trailer parked under a tree. There is no foreseeable end to our endeavours.

Benita and I meet occasionally in the corridor which runs the length of our small flat, and have time only to exchange a curt nod of recognition which is sometimes intercepted, and courteously though mistakenly responded to, by one of the twelve or thirteen honest-smelling and hefty workmen standing about and blocking the way, whose presence in the corridor seems to be connected in some arcane way with the installation of a telephone ordered approximately six months ago.

Our flat is so small that we have to plan to throw something out to make room for anything we might buy. For example, we have no room at all for a gramophone, so I have installed one in the attic with the loudspeaker facing downwards. We hear the sound through the attic door which is left slightly ajar when the weather is not too inclement.

This gives you an idea of the modest nature of our set-up. Even so, our apartment is the envy of all who see it. Such is the housing situation in Switzerland. But while the business of getting fixed up here is a slow and patience-trying process, it is very rewarding in other ways. Besides its obvious ones, Switzerland bestows some very special benefits upon its settlers. Perhaps the most favourable of all is the soothing absence of one-upmanship in the way of life of its people. When I think of the agony you are going through in America with your super-acting-tour-de-force, my heart bleeds for you. Though its residents may be unaware of it, "The American Way of Life" consists almost entirely of one-upmanship, and the pressure upon the individual to engage in it to the full extent of his ability, be he actor, dentist, politician or plain Joe Doakes, is as irresistible as its practice is pernicious, depleting and unhealthy.

Here in Switzerland nobody, not even the President, is anybody in particular. Nobody is trying to become anyone special, nor trying to do anything very noteworthy other than to lead a normal, unhurried, carefree existence. If Swiss people are referred to as being dull, it is because they are so branded by neurotics, who quite understandably find normalcy insupportable.

We enjoy England when we go there, but are never sorry to leave it. The people get you down after a while. I am sorry to say that the War and the dissolution of the British Empire have created among the English people a surly, chip-on-the-shoulder bloody-mindedness all too frequently encountered in their try-and-get-it salesmanship, and their fierce and obdurate chauvinism which is exclusively expressed in terms of anti-Americanism.

Under the therapeutic influence of Benita and Switzerland most of my madness is evaporating. My highest ambition now is to become as dull as any Swiss banker.

The masochistic therapy you have prescribed for yourself on the other hand is probably good for you in your present stage of development, for as Montaigne says, the insights of suffering are essential ingredients of a well-rounded personality. My fondest hope is that you will be able to work out whatever is left of unfinished business in your nervous system and begin to luxuriate with us in the splendour of existential humility. My book will be published in March.

Love

George

RITZ HOTEL
LONDON W.1

Saturday

Dearest Brian,

My spies tell me you had great notices and went off to a flying start, and God knows we need spies since pen-put-to-paper is what you no-bloody-longer seem to put! Anyhow, that's great news no matter how we get it and we are delighted. Fill us in with the details you lazy devil.

England is heaven. The daffodils are popping in the Park and the hedgerows in Kent are beginning to green. The weather of course is ghastly but the Ritz is sunny and warm, and so is Sanders!

We are planting a stake at Billie's house and making the cottage over for ourselves when we are here, and putting in a croquet lawn the size of a county, pushing out the sitting room wall for a piano and generally having a lot of fun. Juliet arrives back tomorrow in a state of hysterical excitement at the prospect. It looks as if we shall be in Rome in May for another picture, then probably back here sometime in July, Aug, and possibly N.Y. in Oct, and you'll be opening about that time won't you? We *do* miss you both. For God's sake don't change your mind about coming over. We have to find somewhere to build in Switzerland between all this hopping about which is none too easy.

We drove back from Lausanne and it was heavenly. Stayed at the spectacular Hotel de la Poste at Avallon, 17th century and looks like a film set, the bedrooms all decorated in butter-coloured satin damask with chandeliers, divine, and *terrific* food and wine. You *have* to try it! [I have tried it since 1928. —B.A.]

I should like to tell you what George is like after all this time with him, but will restrain myself since my feelings are of such unmixed delight and admiration and I have become so violently attached to him that it could only sound like a T.V. commercial. It is all obviously too good to last and I have no doubt Fate is awaiting around the corner with a king-sized bludgeon—although as old age is also just around the corner perhaps no other weapon is necessary!

We see the Eddie Knopfs sometimes, and Sylvia all the time. Betty Bacall I talked to yesterday and she has been burgled to the *bone* absolutely, isn't it too awful. I'm told Peter Viertel has started a divorce so it looks as if the marriage with Deb might go through. Tony is still being a three-dimensional bore about the whole thing, silly ass. Viv got great notices for her *Skin of Our Teeth* T.V. show, which I am ashamed to say we didn't see—so ashamed I haven't had the nerve to call her up! We made Sylvia look at it for us as she was staying home with the flu that night and I may say that she is *still* complaining about us ruining her evening! But as she didn't know and had never even *heard* of the play you can imagine her sense of outrage!

I must stop before this gets long enough to publish. Love to both darlings.

Benita

9

It was not until the spring of 1960 that Katharine Cornell and myself ended our marathon tour of the U.S. in *Dear Liar*, in the course of which we played sixty-seven towns, many of them one-night stands, winding up with a six-week season at the Billy Rose Theater in New York. Traditionally, when theatrical companies went on the road they had traveled by rail, and stars were provided with comfortable, even luxurious private cars which would stand at the station during their engagement in a town and in which they lived, ate and slept. By this time, however, the railroads were no longer navigable and airlines only served big cities, so our company of ten had to ride in a bus or drive rented cars, sometimes for long distances, in order to get from one date to another, eating bad food at lunch counters and sleeping in the nearest motel. It was a tiring way to live, and both tiring and boring for my non-playing wife, who refused to stay at home; but we comforted ourselves with the thought of our impending holiday with George and Benita in Switzerland. At last the show closed. After a few hectic days spent in preparation, we wearily repacked our bag and set out for this long-awaited and anticipated reunion. Unfortunately, however, anticipation is only too often better than realization.

There are no daytime flights to Geneva from New York. The time there being five hours ahead of Eastern Standard Time, the sensible Swiss see no point in working their airport through the night to accommodate American arrivals, so we took off from New York late in the evening. A couple of hours later dinner was served, followed by the inevitable lousy movie, and pretty soon as we moved into another time zone daylight filled the cabin, making any thought of sleep impossible. We got off the plane therefore staggering like drunks with fatigue to find George and Benita awaiting us full of excitement and good cheer. They drove us in George's new Rolls-Royce along the charming coast of the Lake of Geneva to a garden restaurant where we ate a large lunch, accompanied by flagons of Swiss white wine; and then they deposited us at the Beau Rivage Hotel in Ouchy-Lausanne with strict instructions that, after resting, we should be on time for a small dinner party to be given that night at their apartment in our honor. Alas, Fate willed otherwise.

We went to our room, shut off the phone, got out our night things and went to bed, falling instantly into such a deep sleep of exhaustion that we did not wake until the following morning!

The party perforce went on without us, and this inauspicious beginning to our reunion naturally upset them, because their calls to the hotel were met by the statement that we did not wish to be disturbed. However, the bonds of friendship withstood the test and we were made joyful by their evident mutual happiness, since it was obvious that each had brought to the other the qualities which, at that time of their lives, they needed and appreciated. They lived at the same pace, liked the same people, laughed at the same jokes; and, under the influence of Benita's warmth and charm, George was no longer irascible but very amiable, while she in turn was captivated by his eccentricity. She knew what she wanted, she had miraculously found it in George, and she was fiercely loyal to him.

It was during this visit that we were introduced to another person who had come into George's life and whose influence was, alas, to prove of a very different kind than Benita's. Theodore Lowe, an ebullient and persuasive lawyer, whose service with the British Army in Egypt and India had earned for him the decoration of C.B.E., had opened an office in

Lausanne for the practice of international law; and George, recognizing a kindred spirit, had taken to him at once. Together they had hatched a complicated scheme for the avoidance of taxes, which in some way involved the passing of money through Curaçao and Liechtenstein, with its ultimate payment to a Swiss company they had formed under the name of Roturman, S.A., financed of course by George's movie earnings, and of which they were co-directors.

Exciting plans were made for this company, including investment in Swiss real estate, the purchase and storage of Scotch whisky in bulk, Canadian oil wells and other projects about which, it seemed to me, they knew nothing. Lowe began to invest money that had been entrusted to him by clients in various parts of the world, while George bought a new Rolls-Royce and once more talked of abandoning the profession in which he was so phenomenally successful in order to become a business tycoon.

We enjoyed our holiday enormously in quiet, beautiful and orderly Switzerland, and I must admit that it was not difficult to turn a receptive ear to the urging of our dear friends, who begged us to take up residence and join them. As they rightly said, the motion picture business was finished in Hollywood, and the Broadway theater no longer offered satisfactory employment to actors of my standing. In Europe, on the other hand, pictures were being constantly turned out; George had found the move highly profitable and enjoyable, as had David Niven, Bill Holden, James Mason and others, and there seemed to them no reason why I should not do the same.

We returned to California in a state of great indecision, for it is a serious matter to pull up one's roots in a country that has been good to one for twenty-eight years and in which one has made one's home and friends. And yet, when we looked at our beautiful big house and realized that servants to run it were unobtainable, when we faced the huge rise in the cost of maintaining it, and the fact that the movie industry out there was no more, it seemed foolish to pretend that we could continue to live in the style to which we had become accustomed.

Cables pursued us: "Forget idle dreams of theatre. Must become tycoons." "Stop this hesitation. Change your life

Hollywood's "British Colony" broadcast in honor of King George VI and Queen Elizabeth's visit to the U. S. in 1939. Group includes Leslie Howard, Basil Rathbone, Brian Aherne, David Niven, Reginald Gardiner, Roland Young, George Sanders, Ronald Colman, Greer Garson, Nigel Bruce, Sir Cedric Hardwicke, Anna Neagle, Vivien Leigh, Aubrey Smith, Cissie Loftus, Freddie Bartholomew, Radie Harris, Heather Thatcher, Edna Best.

Stag party for Douglas Fairbanks, Jr., when he left Hollywood to join the British Royal Navy. Group includes Brian Aherne, George Sanders, Tom Conway, Reginald Gardiner, Cary Grant, Basil Rathbone, David Niven, Doug, Laurence Olivier, Ronald Colman, Nigel Bruce, Herbert Marshall, Robert Coote, Wing Commander James Adams.

Left, Brian Aherne.

Below, Benita at San Ysidro Ranch, Montecito, 1955.

Opposite above, Ronald and Benita Colman.

Opposite below, Benita Hume on movie set, 1933.

Below, Benita and Ronald Colman with Brian Aherne at San Ysidro Ranch, Montecito, California, circa 1956.

Stuart Hall, Zsa Zsa, George, Bill Shiffren, and Tom Conway, George's brother.

Croquet champion! George receives the Goldwyn Cup from Sam Goldwyn.

Oscar winners: Joseph Mankiewicz, Darryl Zanuck, George Sanders
(*All About Eve*, 1950).

Outside cottage at Weeks, 1960.

Weeks Farm.

Dinner at Weeks, George and Benita.

George in his hour of contemplation!

Summer 1959, French lunch.

Above, George in Villars, 1962.

Right, Eleanor Aherne and Benita at Villars, 1962.

Below, 1960, Verbier in blazing sun!

Above left, Arrival in Cairo; *center,* "Have you actually *tried* to keep a stiff upper lip?"; *right,* "This is a picture of me thinking about Husan. I am going to give you whatever interest I have left in the company as a Christmas present. But consider this—to divert the course of the Nile is a project that some thought worthwhile. But beware! said the Sphinx, such improper hi-jinks might strain my inscrutable smile. Love, George"

Below, "God knows I'm trying to kick the habit, but it's rough!"

Right, "Getting the feel of the place."

Below, "I knew Benita would understand!" In a Cairo night club.

"After five years of marriage!"

"A tycoon at last—if only for TV."

George and Benita at Chemin des Charmettes, Lausanne, 1963.

"Hotel Montejo, 240, Paseo de la Reforma, Mexico, D.F. So here I am, making an ass of myself as usual. Love, George"

Benita, George, and Juliet.

situation and be happy." These were reinforced by persuasive letters.

In the ensuing winter, George's television engagements brought them to California, where they regaled us with exciting descriptions of the success of Roturman, S.A., which had then embarked on a scheme that, in their opinion, held out glittering promises. This was the first time we heard the name of another person who was destined to have a catastrophic effect upon George's life, an obscure English rascal by the name of Albert Harris.

It seemed that Lowe had met this character in his home town of Brighton and had been struck by the commercial possibilities of the story he heard. Harris claimed to have been a pilot in the R.A.F. during the war, though subsequent investigation was to prove that, if indeed he served in that legendary force at all, it was in a very minor ground capacity. According to this story, his wife had bought some excellent sausages from a little local butcher, who, when congratulated on them, said he had found the recipe in a pile of old papers he was cleaning out of the basement of his shop. Attached to the recipe, Harris said, was a letter from Queen Victoria's secretary saying that while on a visit to Brighton Her Majesty had enjoyed these remarkable sausages very much and wished to order some more. As the butcher was on the point of retiring, Harris said, he had taken over the business, concentrating on the sale of "Royal Victoria Sausages" and stimulating trade by putting a copy of Queen Victoria's letter in the window.

Lowe saw great possibilities in the development of this business and suggested it to George as an investment for Roturman, S.A. A company was formed under the name of Cadco Ltd., this being prompted by the title of George's autobiography, *The Memoirs of a Professional Cad*. A factory was leased in Sussex, machinery and workers installed, and contracts were in process of negotiation with railways, schools, institutions and restaurants all over the southern counties for the supply of Royal Victoria Sausages and other meat products. The whole set-up sounded to me reminiscent of Husan Ltd., but perhaps with this in mind, George did not suggest my investing in it, which was just as well.

In the course of 1961, we decided bravely to make the

move to Switzerland. We leased our house in Santa Monica and joined them in Lausanne—a move we have never regretted, although it unfortunately coincided with the collapse of European motion picture production in Spain, Italy and England; and so, apart from three small jobs in London, Vienna and Rome, I did not have George's luck. He, however, continued to work because his unique personality made him valuable in small parts which would otherwise have been ineffective. As usual, he took no interest in them, except for the money they brought in. I once asked him about the part he was to play in a new picture and he replied in a shocked tone, "Oh! I am much too discreet to ask questions like that!"

In answer to a letter in which I mentioned that I had turned down a part in a bad picture, he wrote:

MONTOLIVET 27
LAUSANNE

June 23rd 1961

Dear Brian,

I admire your courage. For an actor to turn down a part, on artistic grounds, in a market such as this, must require a lot of soul-searching. I am glad I shall never have such a problem. I have got to the point where the lousier the part the better I like it. I would find it quite embarrassing to get a really good part nowadays. It would call forth the feeble flames of inner fires long since banked. This is the only part I would be in danger of turning down: the kind I could get my teeth into.

Last night I had some heavy red wine and paid the price with a nuit blanche. But it was not altogether without profit, for, as I lay in bed tossing and turning, I composed the following poem:

Lately, not much has been seen
Of our friend Bishop Fulton J. Sheen.
Where oh where is his flock,

And his frock, and his smock,
And his cock, if you know what I mean.

Love

George

The word he uses in the last line has several meanings in
the U.S. and an additional one in England, a slang word
derived from "poppycock" and meaning nonsense. It is
much used by schoolboys, who might answer a question
about the Headmaster's lecture by saying lightly, "Oh, he
just talked a lot of cock." It is thus used here.

As it turned out, after we settled in Lausanne we did not
see as much of each other as we had hoped, because they
were constantly going away, either to make a picture in another country or to enjoy Weeks Farm in Kent, whereas we
were anchored in Switzerland for our first year by a require-
ment that prospective foreign residents must stay put, after
which, having proved as it were the honesty of their intention, and their general conduct having been observed, they
may receive their Permis de Séjour and are at liberty to travel
—although they are supposed to spend at least six months a
year in the country, a reasonable rule which is not strictly
enforced but gives the Swiss opportunity to eject undesir-
ables.

All countries, of course, have regulations controlling foreign residents, who have, indeed, become a great problem
in the U.S.A. and are rapidly becoming so in the U.K., but
not all deal with it in the same way. Anybody contemplating
foreign residence, therefore, should seek advice from an experienced international lawyer, and in our case he was
George's friend and partner Theodore Lowe.

Plump, roly-poly and jolly, Ted was a likable character, I
thought, although my wife could not take him seriously. I

thought it was apparent that George had given him an exaggerated idea of my wealth, because he immediately began to extol the wonderful possibilities of investments which could be made through their Roturman company, but with my memories of the Husan company I felt no interest. Furthermore, my modest savings had been slowly, sometimes painfully, accumulated through many years under the supervision of an eminent firm of American investment counselors, and I had no intention of gambling them, regarding them as protection for my old age. I had seen enough of the acting profession to know well how necessary this was. I therefore made it clear to Lowe that all I wanted from him was correct advice on my legal position relating to the Swiss and British authorities, and this he gave me.

It is interesting, and I think rather charming, to learn of the special relationship which has existed for so many years between England and the Canton de Vaud, where we had gone to live. It was the British who developed the so-called Swiss Riviera along the shores of the Lake of Geneva, building the hotels, ski resorts and funiculars that made it so popular. Modern young people now go to much higher resorts in the winter; but the British Residents Association still has a large membership, and a genuine feeling of warmth and friendship exists between the Vaudois and the British. We like each other, that's all. We pay our taxes to the Canton, but by a special dispensation, whether written or not I don't know, if we do not choose to divulge the amount of our annual income the Canton will assess us on an amount equivalent to five times our rent! Oddly enough, this seems to work out about right.

Many Swiss ways of doing things are odd when first encountered, but seem to work out all right. Take for instance the political system, which seems very odd indeed to a foreigner. Switzerland is a genuine democracy, but election results do not seem to matter. Ask any Swiss the name of the President: few can tell you. The Constitution is a federal one, like the American, with two houses, but each Canton is in fact a little republic in full control of its own internal affairs, taxes, police, education and so on. Private citizens are entitled to initiate legislation, and any government action which may lead to increased taxation can easily be forced to a referendum of the taxpayers, who usually vote it firmly down.

Until quite recently the majority of the Cantons voted down women's suffrage, and it seems the women were solidly against it on the ground that one vote in the family was quite enough to express its opinion! The Federal Assembly, which sits in Bern, is composed of elected cantonal representatives, who in turn elect the seven members of the government: these belong to various parties, and the balance of this coalition has been worked out carefully, after long strife. The offices of President and Vice-President rotate around the table of this inner circle, which explains why their names escape the memory. Apparently it is felt that the business of government is not to supply "the media" with entertaining or dramatic stories but to govern the country efficiently, and this the Swiss Federal Council does, and it seems to work out all right.

This does not mean, however, that the Swiss like each other. On the contrary, the French, German and Italian Cantons, speaking different languages and having different heritages, distrust each other, and citizens of towns only a few miles apart are likely to detest each other.

I think that perhaps the thing that holds these diverse people together is the fact that, whereas other countries have armies, Switzerland *is* an army. Every Swiss man is a soldier who has to keep his uniform, full kit, gun and ammunition in his house, so that the Army can be mobilized by telephone within forty-eight hours. After finishing his military training, he has to serve in the Reserve one month annually for the rest of his life—in some capacity suitable to his age. When the Swiss hausfrau has finished polishing the floors and door handles, which she does eternally, she gets out her husband's gun and polishes that too, but she resents her husband's military service all the same, because he seems to have such a good time with his old pals up in the mountains, which are well supplied with comforts and honeycombed with recreational facilities.

One can wonder what would happen in other countries if every citizen were given an automatic rifle, a grenade thrower or perhaps some bombs to keep at home, but there again, in Switzerland it seems to work out. In September 1939 all the Swiss passes were fully manned even before Britain declared war on Germany, and today there is no country in Europe where one sees so many soldiers practicing shooting and mountain climbing. When Charlie Chaplin bought his beautiful estate, the Manoir de Ban outside Vevey, he was taking a siesta in his garden on Sunday afternoon when suddenly his peace was shattered by gunfire the other side of his hedge. It was the Swiss Army practicing! It was a long time before Charlie could persuade them to accept another more distant piece of land, which he had to present to them.

Unfortunately, I think George's appreciation of this remarkable country was limited to its economic advantages, so that he did not see its interest or its beauty. When he had completed, most efficiently, his work on their apartment in Lausanne, electrifying all the clocks, installing complicated sound systems in the attic, building bookshelves illuminated from hidden sources and so on, he began to groan about the lack of a garden with a lawn on which he could play, and teach us, his favorite game of croquet. This went on until we were dismayed by the thought that they might pull out of Lausanne, leaving us high and dry, as it were. Benita, who by now was utterly devoted to him, sympathized with him and actually was so happy at Weeks Farm with her sister and daughter that I believe she would have been quite content to reside there and pay whatever taxes were asked of her, but I knew George so well and was so accustomed to his abrupt changes of his life plans that I determined to find something that would hold him, and I made an effort to interest him in golf.

In the hills behind Lausanne we have a beautiful course, Le Golf de Lausanne, always referred to in English as "the Golf," of which I had become an enthusiastic member. I made all my friends at the Golf which, in the true Swiss way, is run in eccentric fashion. It is a sort of miniature United Nations, the membership being composed of many nationalities, but neither the President nor the Secretary speaks anything but French, and members who have been there for forty years have no idea who is on the Committee. The clubhouse is neither as stark as those in Britain nor as luxurious as those in America, but it is well run and is definitely the social center of the area.

I called George and invited him to play. At first, he would not hear of the idea, but when I promised we would play in the morning, when few are out, and would not go more than nine holes, he reluctantly agreed to think about it.

A little later, he called back. "I'll come if you will pick me up and if I can play in shorts and bare feet," he announced.

I shuddered to think what the members might say, for shorts are not worn and as for bare feet—! However, for me the stakes were high, and I thought this might be at least the thin edge of the wedge, so I took the chance and agreed. Next morning, I picked him up. He was dressed in shorts, an old cotton shirt and a pair of bedroom slippers.

I had borrowed a set of clubs for him and arranged for caddies to meet us at the tenth tee, which is hidden from the clubhouse. The caddies were teenage girls, whom we get from the local school, and very efficient they are, pulling the bags on golf carts—*chariots* in French—and showing considerable knowledge of the game. George refused his at once. He only needed one club, he said, and borrowed my five iron.

I teed up my ball and sliced it into the trees. George struck his firmly down the center of the fairway, and as we strode away he took off his shirt and slippers and stuffed them into my bag, continuing in shorts only. I glanced apprehensively back at the clubhouse.

Well, he was on the green in three and I was there in five. He refused the use of my putter but was very artful with the five iron and won the hole. George one up. I was over the green at the short eleventh and he was on. George two up. We halved the twelfth, and I lost my ball in the long grass at the thirteenth. George three up. At the fifteenth, I put my second shot into the lake, incurring a two-stroke penalty— and so it went. With his one club he beat me, affecting all the time to be bored with such a silly game.

I had planned to take him direct from the eighteenth green to the car in the parking area, but he claimed a drink as the winner, so we had to go into the bar. I insisted that he put on the shirt and slippers before doing so. Fortunately the luncheon crowd had not yet arrived and the bar was almost empty, so after he had downed a couple of large vodkas I was able to ease him out of the side door and into the car. That was the end of our golf together.

The Sanderses now spent as much time as possible in Kent, going back and forth by road in George's Rolls-Royce. This involved a trip of 450 miles, not counting the time occupied by crossing the Channel whether by ferry from Calais or by airlift from Le Tourquet, and as George refused to drive faster than forty miles per hour or to use any autoroute, they were always looking for luxurious and charming places in which to stay in France. It was thus that George developed the idea that they must buy a house on the river Yonne, a small tributary of the Seine. "A place on the Yonne" became his dream. A small place with a garden and lawn beside the river in which they could install that legendary French couple who would look after it, and who would presumably always be ready to greet them with smiles and a good French dinner. In vain we told them that such a couple was unobtainable and even if they were they would soon come to regard the place as their own and would resent the occasional arrival of the owners. The French are not that devoted to foreigners, and we did not believe the natives would be friendly, so we tried both reason and ridicule, calling it "Yonder Chateau" and "Hither and Yonne," but the dream persisted and it was almost two years before they abandoned it and decided instead to find a house near Beauvais in the flat, uninteresting country between Paris and Amiens. They actually went there for a week to look around but came back very disillusioned.

I never understood how George could reconcile this dream with the fact that all his fortunes were tied up with Theodore Lowe and their Roturman company in Lausanne, not to speak of the taxation dangers he would incur by owning a residence in another country. In the end, however, the dream faded because he became so much in demand for pictures in other parts of the world. In her letters, Benita indicates her growing lack of enthusiasm for these foreign locations.

Monday

Darlings,

The most glorious long letter from you Brian this morning. I suffered—but without surprise—over your experience with the Swiss doctors. Perhaps we should abandon this naive belief in their favour. Actually this isn't limited to Switzerland: in America they either won't make house calls or do so very reluctantly and at great expense. Oh no, you have to make an appointment two weeks ahead and in the middle of lunchtime, at the office, where you are grilled by a secretary who wants to know every detail of your family life and financial standing, after which the great man greets you with all the inspiring charm of a man selling stamps in an English Post Office, and about as much talent. It's very discouraging.

George left for Budapest last week and I shall follow to-morrow. This long parting, as I am sure you know, is agony to my uxorious nature. I think I am as bad as Queen Victoria who said of her Albert "I am never 'à mon aise' when he is not *in the room.*"

I don't know what the picture is that George is doing, and he of course would not consider apprising himself of this superfluous information, but Bennie Thau of all people is involved, and Dick Thorpe and Buddy Hackett and Cooter, and we shall be there about two months at the Gellert Hotel as far as I have managed to glean. And they are paying my fare which I think very handsome of them.

Poor Profumo! He turned out to be a very poor carpenter, didn't he? One screw and the whole Cabinet fell apart!

Oh, don't go to California! Can't you get someone to house-sit for a bit? It's such a sweat getting there isn't it, and

105

both sea and air are so rough at this time of the year. Wait for us and go in the spring.

Isn't Cadco terrific! Everyone keeps making dark remarks and offering the gloomiest wishes for its success, all of which begin with "Well, I hope—!" But we think it madly exciting and feel very proud. Lord Linlithgow thinks so too and may be joining us. Of course we're not at the winning post yet, but it's in sight and the suspense is terrific! George didn't want to do the picture of course, but we felt it was tempting providence to turn all that money down, if you know what I mean? Have to finish packing now. Lots of love to both and we are so glad that you are at least a bit better.

Benita

10

All my life I have been thrilled by the names of famous
trains. The Orient Express from Paris to Istanbul, the Train
Bleu rushing through the night to the Riviera, the Flying
Scotsman and the Brighton Belle rolling north and south
from London, the Twentieth Century Limited, the Santa Fe
Chief and Super Chief crossing the vast continent of America
—these were magical names to people of my generation, but
on a dark November evening in 1963 the rather dingy train
awaiting us in the Zurich station offered no interest until, at
a second glance, I noticed that under the grime it bore a
name in letters which had once been of polished brass—the
Wiener Waltzer! My spirits rose. How charming, how romantic and how right, I thought, for I was on my way to
Vienna to play the part of Johann Strauss in a picture to be
made by Walt Disney.

Why I should have been offered this job was something I
could not fathom, for I was obviously miscast, but the prospect of six weeks in Vienna at the fabled Sacher Hotel was
too alluring to be missed. Memories of Alfred Lunt and Lynn
Fontanne in *Reunion in Vienna* and of Carol Reed's *The Third
Man* came back to me as I lay in my stone-hard berth while
the Wiener Waltzer rattled and bounded through the night.
I thought of the Emperor Franz Josepf and his tragic, beautiful Empress Elizabeth, of Schönbrunn, Mayerling and the
ill-fated Rudolf, of the Winterhalter portraits, the famous
Opera House, the Lippizaner horses, the boys choir singing

in the Palace Chapel and of Djemel's famous coffee house—so many exciting and nostalgic experiences awaiting my wife and myself.

We rumbled into the Vienna station on a bitterly cold, dark and drizzling November morning and found a warm welcome awaiting us on the platform from the producer of the picture and his assistants. Both the drizzle and the warmth were to continue throughout our stay. Sacher's ushered us into a suite which indeed seemed like a replica of a set from *Reunion in Vienna*, and after breakfast and a bath I was driven out to the ramshackle old studio on the edge of town in which the picture was to be shot. My first question was about the length of my engagement, since the part, though effective, was confined to the first half of the picture, and I could not understand why they should need six weeks of my services. Oh, they said, that was simple. I would spend the first two weeks learning to play the violin, and the other four I would, on the requisite days, be working on the set.

Learning to play the violin? What was this? Apart from a few years' drudgery at the piano in my extreme youth and some singing lessons in later life, I had no musical education and was staggered by the idea! No problem, they assured me. I would only have to learn three short passages and how to conduct a few bars while the camera was on me; and an eminent violinist, Professor Babinsky, had been engaged to teach me. He was also teaching the young actor who was to play my son, and who had nine passages to learn, so there was nothing to worry about. With that, I was led to the make-up department, not a modern well-equipped, brilliantly lighted, chromium-plated department such as I had known in the Hollywood Studios, but a dark little room, sparsely furnished with a rickety old table and chair and a cracked mirror, over which hung a couple of naked electric bulbs.

I sat in the chair and waited until the make-up man came in, a shy and rather seedy-looking old fellow. We regarded each other, he with diffidence and I with distrust. He spoke no English and I no German. We communicated by signs and a few words of imperfect French. He opened a drawer crammed with bits of crepe hair, ancient bottles of spirit gum, broken combs and half-squeezed tubes of greasepaint and extracted a photograph of Johann Strauss, which he carefully placed against the mirror. He then rummaged about in some boxes under the table and produced a black wig and large mustache, which he placed proudly before me. I looked at them, and at him, and then we both contemplated the photograph in silence.

My God, I thought, what have I let myself in for? Accustomed as I was to complete reliance upon the tremendous technical competence of Hollywood, I felt unnerved. I leaned forward and studied the picture again. There could be no doubt. I could never, with all the aids of make-up, look remotely like the elder Johann Strauss. Why had I come, and what should I do? The obvious thing was to admit my mistake, persuade the Disney company to tear up my contract, and board the Wiener Waltzer that night. I looked again at the make-up man, who gave me a timid smile. Oh, what the hell, I thought. At least let the poor old chap have a go at it!

Half an hour later he stepped back and gestured toward the mirror. I stared in astonishment, for I was completely transformed! Johann Strauss looked back at me. Indeed the famous Westmore Brothers of Hollywood could not have achieved a more startling result. Excitedly I called in the producer and director, and we all stood admiring my reflection in the cracked mirror. Confident that I could look the part at least, I forgot the Wiener Waltzer and returned happily to the nostalgic charm of the Sacher Hotel.

Next morning I visited the set, where work was already in progress, and was introduced to the cast, after which I was taken upstairs to meet my teacher, Professor Babinsky. The professor's English was heavily accented and barely comprehensible.

"Pliz," he said, "you play ze violon?"

"Nein," I answered.

"Nicht . . . at all?" he asked in astonishment.

"Nein!" I repeated firmly. I thought it best to be frank.

He shook his head in dismay, as indeed he might. Then he picked up a violin and bow and handed them to me. "Pliz," he said, "let me see vat you do."

I shoved the instrument under my chin and drew the bow

across the strings, producing a horrible squawk. Shuddering, the professor took it from me.

"Nein! Nein! Nein!" he groaned, and we stared at each other in silence, two minds with but a single thought. Then he put down the violin, motioned me to a chair and left the room. I knew where he had gone, to see the producer and to tell him that it was impossible, in two weeks, to teach anyone who did not even know how to hold a violin to play like Johann Strauss. After a while, he came back sighing deeply and proceeded to show me how to hold the thing and how to draw the bow back and forth across the strings. For the next few days that room became a torture chamber for us both.

As a small boy, I used to struggle to learn the trick of patting my head with one hand while rubbing my tummy with the other, but that was indeed child's play compared to the contortions necessitated by the violin. It looks easy, but try it! Plant the blunt end of the thing firmly against the neck, turn the head hard left and clamp down with the chin —a painful procedure in my case because of an old injury between the third and fourth cervical vertebrae—while the left hand supports the thin end, where of course the fingers must move up and down and across the strings, pressing upon the exact spots necessary to produce the desired notes. Meanwhile, right elbow lifted, the bow is passed smoothly, and exactly at right angles, across the selected strings. Professor Babinsky started me off with the simple scale, which I practiced—squawk . . . sqeak . . . squawk . . . sqeak . . . sqeak—slowly, laboriously and with desperation, hour after hour. The pain at the back of my neck became acute. I would return to the hotel looking over my left shoulder, and felt that I would never hold my head straight again; indeed I could feel the effects months later. All the while, the professor regarded me gloomily, wincing from time to time as I struggled on.

Finally, unable to bear the torture any longer, I went down to the set and spoke to Steve Previn, the director. Get yourself another boy, I told him. The task was impossible. After four days, I couldn't even play a simple scale.

He roared with laughter. "My God!" he cried, "I don't

want you actually to *play* the damned thing—of course not!
All the music will be dubbed in by experts anyway. Make
them give you a violin with rubber strings. All I want is to
see you pushing the bow up and down, roughly in time with
the music, which you will hear over the playback on tape. If
any of it doesn't look too good, we can always cut away from
you to shots of the orchestra. Don't worry at all. There is no
problem!"

Happily I grabbed an interpreter and bounded back to the
professor. Rubber strings? He was horrified! Why, the bow
would slide sideways on them and musicians would see it.
They would also see at once that my bowing was not authentic in any way. Oh no-no, it would never do! To hell with
musicians, I thought. They would make up a very small part
of Walt Disney's audience, most of whom would be young-
sters watching the picture on television. Anyway, we had
only ten days left, so it was rubber strings or nothing.

Day after day I made the poor man play a passage over
and over on his fine instrument while I followed him on my
faked one, until I felt confident that I could fool anybody but
an expert; but I never worked so hard or suffered so much in
my acting career.

The great moment arrived when, in my wonderful make-
up and costume, I strode into the ballroom, pushed my way
through the dancers, ascended the podium, snatched the violin angrily from my son's hands and, using the bow as a
baton, conducted the orchestra in "Tales from the Vienna
Woods." Out of the corner of my eye I could see the orchestra
laughing at me, but at the correct moment, as the lilting
music blared from the playback, I turned my back on them,
faced the beautiful ballroom crowded with costumed extras,
and launched into my solo passage *con brio*. As the famous
waltz crashed to its triumphant end, the whole set burst into
applause, and over the loudspeaker I heard Previn shouting,
"Fantastic! Marvelous!" Carried away by this tumultuous
reception, filled with pride and excitement, and oblivious to
the fact that no cameras were turning at the rehearsal and
that these were only paid actors, I transferred my bow to my
violin hand, place my right hand on my heart and bowed
repeatedly like Johann Strauss himself.

Suddenly I became aware of Professor Babinsky standing ashen-faced below me.

"Oh pliz!" he pleaded desperately. "At least finish on ze E string!"

Well, as is the way of movies, we did not shoot the scene that day. First it was necessary to do "reverse shots" of the ballroom, and much time had to be spent arranging the lights, placing the cameras, and getting several hundred people on their chalk marks. Finally a first rehearsal of the waltz was attempted. The playback record was started over the loudspeaker and Previn cried, "Action!" I began my conducting, and the dancers, all in authentic and beautiful costumes of Vienna in the 1880s, stumbled around the floor.

"Stop! Stop!" shouted Previn. The music stopped. There was a short conference between the choreographer and director while we all waited to hear what was wrong. Then he left his perch by the camera and, megaphone in hand and assistants following behind, came down on the floor.

"Nobody is waltzing!" he boomed. "This is a great ball in Vienna a hundred years ago, and Johann Strauss is conducting. Don't any of you know how to waltz?" Apparently nobody did. The extras stared at him dumbly. Neither war nor Russian occupation had prepared them for that sort of thing. Shooting stopped for the day and a desperate search ensued. Toward evening, somebody had the idea of calling the Opera House, where the ballet master immediately provided a solution of our problem. Whenever the Opera needed expert waltzers on stage they used a particular group of young aristocrats who delighted in dancing for them. They were known as the "Edel Statisten—the Nobly Born."

Two days later, I again rehearsed my dramatic entrance, pushing my way not through a crowd of professional extras but of handsome young gentlemen and beautiful young ladies who waltzed divinely, with verve and precision. Nor was this the only difference, for instead of regarding their presence as just another boring day's work, they fell immediately under the spell of the opulent set and the lovely music and behaved as if they were at a glorious party in old Vienna.

By ten o'clock, champagne corks were popping in the loges surrounding the dance floor, and laughter, seldom heard on a movie set, was filling the air. Impeccably dressed young men were standing before me clicking their heels, bowing and offering me a glass with which to drink a toast. Lovely young girls were throwing me captivating smiles as they whirled around, and the whole illusion was so complete that I felt indeed I was Johann Strauss himself. After the champagne ran out, and after we had all eaten the heavy and badly cooked lunch in the dirty cafeteria, it must be admitted that the illusion faded, and as the assistant director cried, "Once more! Once more!" again and again, the smiles faded too.

On the second day of shooting the same scene, it was announced that alcohol would not be permitted on the set, but by that time the Edel Statisten had discovered the truth about extra work in the movies—it is monotonous, repetitious and intolerably boring. Their beautiful manners, however, were unfailing. A small deputation of four came to ask if I would honor them by attending a party which they would like to give in my honor at the end of the picture. I looked at their youth and beauty sadly.

"My dears," I said, "I am afraid you will be very disappointed. I shall look very different and much older. I shall not have my wig—and I shall bring my wife!" Charming smiles, clicking heels, bows and curtseys. They would be delighted, and it would indeed be an honor to meet my wife.

My last day's work was a short one, and provided an unexpected shock which jolted me out of my state of euphoria about old Vienna. I was driven to the Studio as usual by a young Austrian in threadbare clothes who looked as if he needed a good meal, and on the way he suggested that, as I was leaving early, he would like to drive me through the famous woods and take me to a high point from which there was a wonderful view of the city. This did not sound very attractive on a dank, dark winter's day, but to please him I casually agreed, thinking I would leave too late anyway.

During the morning I had to go to the office to pick up quite a large sum of money due to me for my living expenses. Expecting to be given a check, I was surprised when the secretary asked me to wait a few minutes, as the driver had gone to the Bank to pick up cash. He soon returned and handed her a paper bag containing a large wad of bills, which she carefully counted as he stood there. Then she gave me a big pile, which, with some difficulty, I stuffed into my pocket. This seemed an unusual way to handle such a matter, but I signed the receipt and thought no more about it.

My wife came out that afternoon to help me pack my things and say goodbyes. It was raining as we got into the car, and the driver turned his head in surprise when he saw her. "Oh—madame come too?" he asked. I laughed. Yes, I said as we sat down and closed the door, and we would like to go back to the hotel please. After a moment's hesitation, he asked if we could give a lift to a friend of his who wanted to go into town. Certainly, we said. The driver beckoned, and a big muscular figure moved quickly from the shadow of the wall and jumped into the front seat of the car. As we drove off, I looked at the back of his thick neck, and when he turned a little I saw that he had a great scar down one side of his face and a couple of front teeth missing. Suddenly I felt uneasy. We drove in silence for a while and then the car swung off the main road and began a winding climb toward the hills.

"Where are you going?" I asked sharply.

He muttered something in German, which I don't understand.

My wife, however, speaks it fluently. "He says he is taking us up to see the view," she told me.

But it was too late for that, I exclaimed! It was nearly dark, rain was falling, and we were climbing through woods into a thick mist. The two men muttered together. Fear gripped me. What a fool I had been, what a crazy fool! Of course, he had seen me put all that money into my pocket. My wife didn't know about that. We were in danger. We were in grave danger! I felt my wife's hand gripping mine, and surreptitiously I passed the wad of bills to her. With no sign of surprise, she slipped it under her coat. As we wound upward through the trees, the headlights reflected from the mist that enveloped us.

And now my Eleanor, although we had not exchanged a word, rose to the challenge; leaning forward, she began to speak to the men in German, rapidly, gaily and almost hysterically, telling them funny stories, laughing and behaving as though we four were the best of friends. The car turned into a dead end among the trees and stopped. I saw the two men exchange glances. Now it comes, I thought. I am not much of a fighter and would have small chance of defending both of us. Were they armed? Probably. We would give them the money, but would they drive off and leave us there, or would they think it necessary to kill us? For a few moments they sat in silence, occasionally replying to Eleanor in monosyllables. Her unexpected presence and the fact that she spoke German obviously disconcerted them.

Finally the driver muttered something to his companion and then told Eleanor it was too dark to see the view. We would come again, he said, another time. Swiftly he turned the car and drove back to the city, Eleanor keeping up her flow of conversation all the way and eliciting only an occasional grunt from the front seat. At the hotel we gôt out, thanked them cordially and said good night. Without a word, they vanished into the darkness, and we were never so glad to see the back of anybody. We heard later that neither they nor the Studio car were ever seen again.

That evening, still in a state of shock, we went to the party given in our honor by our young friends the Edel Statisten. It was a "Heurigen," the traditional Austrian celebration of the new wine, a barrel of which stood in the center of the room. Flowers and autumn foliage decorated the walls, and plain, tasty country food lay on the candlelit tables. Soft, youthful voices, gentleness and gaiety filled the old house. We spoke no word of our terrifying adventure, allowing ourselves to be soothed by the warmth and charm of the hour. The old Austria still lives, despite the wars, the years of poverty and suffering, the Nazi and Communist occupations, the misery, bloodshed and starvation: that one nostalgic evening proved it to us.

Next day, we again boarded the Wiener Waltzer and rattled home to reality. I never saw Professor Babinsky again, and for anyone who knows anything about the making of movies it is perhaps unnecessary to add that, while I was shown conducting the orchestra for a few bars, not one foot of my violin playing ever appeared on the screen.

Monday

Well darlings,

I guess that *Lawrence of Arabia* was worse as a location. Maybe. But I could really send your first letter from Vienna right back to you because it expresses exactly what we are getting here! O dear me, the dismal trials of the Socialist experiments: the grey paint flaking sadly down like London snow, the pitiful commissionaire at the entrance tottering about in an unbuttoned uniform clearly made about 1912, no decent drink—except Scotch thank God—a bar so dirty that one hesitates to sit down and a frowzy barmaid to fix what few concoctions she can. They all talk about going to Vienna as if it were paradise which is rather funny! Things are getting better they say, more cars, more freedom, more building —but *meanwhile!* That's the thing! George did his usual thing of asking to see the best room they had in the place and then sending for the Manager and demanding the best suite, on the ground that the rooms were uninhabitable. He does this everywhere we go, reducing Managers to trembling apologies and me to deep embarrassment, but here I must say there was solid ground for his behaviour and we did wind up with a fair-sized suite decorated in all the rainbow hues of cow-pat colours and with the *odd*est beds. They are made, for some inscrutable reason, in three sections. The joins are more in the nature of steps than joins and it takes quite a bit of agility to stay aboard at all—and "aboard" is the word because it is *dead* hard and surmounted by a *huge* perfectly unattached duvet thing so that you have the impression of sleeping on the floor and pulling the bed up over you.

We have just come back from a perfectly ghastly meal of stuffed cabbage, so divine in Calif and absolutely lethal in its home town.

There's no question but what Socialism just isn't worth the price of a visa. It's bloody awful, 3rd rate and dismal. No room for the gifted, the colourful or the indigenous talents, just a lousy imitation of capitalism.

For God's sake write! The frills of the Iron Curtain are chafing our knees and we are planning the most exotic trips to the Bahamas in ships with silken sails to offset our present tribulations.

I brought your letter out to George which of course he loved—your typewriter upset Billie though, because when I said "I have a fat letter from Brian," she said angrily "Where? I didn't see it!" Up to now she has confined herself to reading the postcards but delivering the letters *by hand* so that she can read them the same time we do! But if we weren't there I think she would be strongly tempted to open it first! We shall be here for *weeks*—isn't it hell.

Lots of love from both to both,

Benita

The picture came to an end at last, and they returned to England, but George was soon off to make another in Israel, of all places.

ACCADIA GRAND HOTEL
FULLY AIR-CONDITIONED
TEL-AVIV

Thursday

Darlings,

Well, we took off on El Al. We seem to use the damnedest airlines, and this one with all those strange letters which I find so un-nerving, don't you, and when we bumped down at Frankfort I thought the pilot was more of an L than an AL type too. Anyhow we arrived safely and rather privately, in as much as there were only two other passengers. This place is on the sea and climate-wise very Californian. There is a very large pool which has a lot of class—all lower—and a

117

great many people, and it is integrated as all hell. The sunshades are fringed with lyrics extolling the local shops, you know the kind of thing, and pseudo-American short orders being served. George explained crossly to the waiter that he didn't like frankfurters and demanded *pork* sausages. "You know—PORK!" he insisted. I sometimes wonder what goes on inside that head.

I haven't been into town yet but George did this afternoon and his report was something less than rapturous, but I'll have to go and have a mouse around tomorrow. Dear me, six weeks *does* seem a long time doesn't it! I'm afraid I'm going to feel very traitorous leaving after three!

I do wish you and Bill Frye had come down to Weeks that Sunday. It was really divinely beautiful, what with the roses and the doves, and Billie had baked the most marvellous bread. It was idyllic, that's what, and we now play croquet all over the far fields to the constant amazement of the sheep who are our riveted audience.

Keep in mind that letters will be hysterically welcome.

Lots of love and from G.

Benita

ACCADIA GRAND HOTEL
FULLY AIR-CONDITIONED
TEL-AVIV

Saturday

Darlings,

No question but we have had enough of it. I don't see how this place can amount to anything unless it gets rid of this crazy religious group which apparently calls the tune of the country. The *most* religious sect, which I guess is what the Orthodox Jews feel to be the most admirable, takes quite a bit of believing. Their beards are *colossal*, right down to here and out to there, and then they have very long curls down each side and surmount this whole unlovely picture with large flat beaver hats. When they marry, their wives, presumably in a state of shock, shave their heads bald as a knee

—with a fine disregard for the hazards of knowing which way up a person is in the dark of the night. And if you should visit their quarter by day (Shabotu) they will shout at you, and stone you, and lie in front of your car, hoping, I suppose, by these cogent arguments and rational examples to convert you so that you will go home and grow a beard of your own! And this is a new country!

The Kosher food is insisted on everywhere—to the extent that they have Government men *watching* both the kitchens and the dining rooms—it drives you up the wall. If you have meat or chicken, you can't have butter or cheese, except in another room. You can't have cream in your coffee even, or a glass of milk with a chicken sandwich! I mean what makes them think any non-Jew is going to spend any time in such a mad-house? The paradox is that the young people aren't religious at *all*. We saw a wedding in a Kibbutz the other day and when two couples exchanged a few remarks and had a drink with a young man in shirtsleeves, that was it! No Rabbis or anything of the kind! They were married!

I'll come back next week but I feel terrible leaving George here. It's really suicidal on these bloody locations, isn't it. We went to the sea of Galilee yesterday and had a little walk, on the water of course. It's very like a crumby California really. The Kirk Douglases are here and rather jolly we think, and a nice tenor from the Opera called Da Costa, but otherwise the hotel is full of *monsters!* I'll give you a blow directly I get in, it'll be the 14th or 15th I think.

Lots of love

Benita

.

After a short stay in Lausanne, where at last we four were able to meet, George was engaged for another picture, this time in Egypt. We never saw any of these pictures, nor, I am sure, did he; but he got handsomely paid for them—or his Roturman company did. Benita's letters from Cairo were as usual undated, but from the envelopes I would guess they were written in April-May 1964. The opening sentence of this one is written in imitation Arabic script.

NILE HILTON
CAIRO, EGYPT, U.A.R.

Friday

Darlings,
We can't distinguish this place from Osaka, Japan. All cities look alike nowadays, and awful is what they all look. The only difference here is that through the inevitable high box apartment buildings you can see the Pyramids which is exciting—if you are prone to excitement about that class of thing. We dutifully drove out to see them this afternoon, but the moment you set foot out of the car you are engulfed by a crowd of ghastly types wanting you to ride their beastly camels which are standing around like a lot of conceited spinsters draped in dirty shawls and sneering at everyone. I thought the Sphinx was showing her age and had the dispirited, threadbare air of one who is fed up with trying to keep the sand out of her ears. I really hate the exploited wonders of the world: there is no hope of finding a second in which you can shut the guides up and have a little wonder on your own.

We are surprised to see what handsome people the Arabs are, marvellous gay open sort of faces and—in spite of my apprehensions—they flew the plane in like a feather, no problem at all except that we were over two hours late starting, but then that's always happening with air travel.

Its very hot but nice and the hotel is air-conditioned. Full of cold air and hot Americans. George is looking for an Arabian Stewpot [Nickname for Stuart Hall. —B.A.] and a fez with which to take "Old" Cairo by storm. He has already given much more satisfaction to the tourists than they are likely to get at the Museum, judging by the stares and loud remarks which greet his progress across the lobby!

I didn't want to leave Lausanne. It was lovely with you two there and that is what I really enjoy. "Abroad" is a great strain I think and very little pleasure. I wish to God that famous Hilton hospitality would get our vodkas the hell up here, I think they're sending it up the Nile on a barge. Lots of love. Hope Madrid is nice and spring-like.

Benita

At this time, having returned from a visit to Spain, we were busily engaged in decorating our small rented apartment in a charming but somewhat dilapidated old house in Lausanne, and Benita was very interested in our progress. Meanwhile Ted Lowe and his wife, Martha—carried away by the glittering promise of Roturman, S.A., and Cadco Ltd.—were building an enormous mansion on the side of a mountain not far from the famous Victorian Hotel Beau Rivage at Ouchy. Benita refers to it as the Lowe Rivage in her second letter from Egypt.

NILE HILTON
CAIRO, EGYPT, U.A.R.

Tuesday

Ellie darling,
I can't believe that silly son-of-a-bitch Moinart did them in lavender! Oh my God, after all that trouble and choosing and waiting—isn't it the boiling *end*. What are you going to do about it? Is it by any improbable chance a pretty lavender? Anyway it's the most fugitive colour of the lot, and goes grey practically instantly. I don't know why one *ever* expects *anything* to come out right. Can you imagine what Pixie is going through at the Grand Palais de Lowe Rivage!
Isn't it a bore Europe is having such a miserable cold spring—your letter rather took the crimp out of our Spanish plans! Of course this is the most fabulous climate night and day, but dry dry dry. It doesn't have all the lush green gardens of Calif—not only doesn't have *all*, doesn't have *any*—

121

and no dew, not even a drop, so one gets to feel pretty much like a rusk. It would really be a paradise if it had beautiful white Moorish type palazzos and gardens and fountains and swimming pools and those beautiful white ibis flying around but that is not in fact the situation which prevails.

Being hard put to it to amuse ourselves, and George currently working all night, we decided to have a little sail on the Nile yesterday in one of those lateen sailboats, so pretty they are. You should have seen the Captain. He looked just like Doug Fairbanks in his splendid waistcoat and sash and turban and voluminous black Turkish trousers over his bare brown ankles and feet. Really a marvellous get-up. It was too bad he fell in as we pushed off, but I don't think anybody would have noticed much except for the awning—I never did understand how he managed to pull that in with him. But anyway, it all gave a lot of pleasure to a sizeable crowd of children who expressed their appreciation by loud cries and jeers, and indeed took such a good view of the proceedings that they formed an immediate resolution to accompany us alongside in rowboats. I can't say this was exactly what we had in mind—you might say our trip came out rather lavender too!

God knows when this letter may reach you, but if by chance it is next week then Juliet and her friend Missy Bolton will be at the flat and I told her to call you because she wants advice on what to do for her R.A.D.A. Shakespearean test— this is for you Brian—I thought the Henry the Fifth scene in which he woos the French Princess (which Ronnie and I thought you did better than anybody) but she has some idea of doing a very boring Volumnia one just because it is more obscure—and rightly so—and I want you to put your nose in.

Did you say you were thinking of going down to Italy before going to England? Our plane stops at Rome and we think it would be nice if we met up in the Piazza di Spagna wouldn't it?! May 13, 14, 15 about.

Three more weeks! Terrible to wish one's life away, but I'm not sure living in a hotel can be called life! I'm going to a dinner party tonight but G. is working dammit, and to-morrow we are invited to another one which maybe will be interesting—it has to be better than room service anyway!

Harriette Little has become my constant correspondent since meeting at your house and here. She's really very sweet isn't she—I think she was quite distressed at my prospects here, and avec beaucoup de raison il faut dire!! Well, it's time for me to race downstairs. It now being Saturday and 5 o'clock I shall be just in time for the Thursday papers.

Lots of love from both to both.

Benita

We drove down to meet them in Rome and I remember that the four of us dined with a charming titled Italian couple in a smart restaurant. Benita whispered to me that our hostess, the Contessa, was of Russian origin and was George's sister, and this surprised me, because she bore no resemblance whatever to the very English sister who had been in California during the war. I remarked on this at dinner, whereupon there was a distinct impression of uneasiness around the table and the conversation was quickly changed. As we were leaving, Benita murmured in my ear, "She is . . . well . . . a sort of *half* sister to George, dear—but don't bring it up!"

Just what is a "sort of half sister"? we wondered. As far as we knew, there had been no divorce or previous marriage in George's family, and we could only conclude that the Contessa must have been the result of an indiscretion on the part of Sanders Senior. She was "born the wrong side of the sheets," as the saying goes. Anyway, after that we referred to her as "George's friend," and all was well.

That autumn we drove across France to Le Touquet, airlifted our car into Kent, and stayed at lovely old Weeks Farm, where we heard more about heavy investments and ambitious plans for Cadco Ltd. and Royal Victoria Sausages. In the privacy of the garden, I put a few searching questions to George, who brushed them off impatiently. No, he said, he never visited the factory at Brighton, although it was less than an hour away. That was quite unnecessary, as he had absolute faith in Harris. Benita, though pouring all her available money into the company, seemed totally ignorant of its operation. This too was quite unnecessary as she had absolute faith in George. In any case, both were fully occupied at that time in building and decorating extra rooms at Weeks, a charming cottage for themselves, another for Benita and Billie's mother, and transformation of the gatehouse and barn into guest rooms with baths, all soon to be needed for Juliet's twenty-first birthday party, which we had come over to attend. Guests were also housed at a large hotel near Canterbury. Food was supplied by Fortnum & Mason, and a band was brought down from London.

We will divorce you if you don't come [Benita had written]. Don't stay in Le Touq. It's all shut. Come here. We'll get you in somewhere. Actually I don't know *who*'s coming except Viv and Sylvia Ashley—Fairbanks—Gable—Djordjadze and about 120 others. Syl is going to Calif in Jan and I have given her our servants who are thrilled to death, although between us I don't think it will be long before that honeymoon is over! She is such a disorganised dame, much as I dote on her. I can't imagine how she figured she could run a house out there without any help *or* any furnishings. I mean you *know* the curtains will never get made and she will buy four birdcages and some gold forks but never get around to the Hoover, the dustbin or an extra light bulb!

I will give you Bunny's book on arthritis and you shall eat cod liver oil, sardines and salmon, and wear a copper bracelet and be perfectly cured of hyper-acidity which I regard as a tiresome remark meaning nothing at all. "Incipient ulcer" is questionable too, because they have enough trouble diagnosing a great rollicking ulcer: it seems too acute to find one which hardly has its toe in the door. Still, if that is really the case, you should probably go back to the ranch and start building mud walls very slowly in the sun, very pleasant and therapeutic, and then you can have a nice lean on it now and then which will be relaxing! At any rate, it is a great deal more rewarding than driving visitors to Gruyère three times a week which is enough to give anyone stomach cramps!

I am dying to be in America again. We thought we'd go and look at Mexico. I've never been there.

The party was a huge success and seemed to go on all night. Everybody sang—an expensive cast. George played the piano, Judy Garland and Liza Minelli sang, and a rather drunken game of croquet went on outside in the moonlight, while the young danced with inexhaustible energy. Some of the guests left in broad daylight to drive all the way back to London. Oh yes, a huge success, but it took us a couple of days lying in the garden to recover, and then all too soon we had to return to Lausanne, close our apartment and pack up for the long journey to our house in Santa Monica, California, on which our tenant's lease was about to expire.

This had come to be our annual custom, it seemed, and I was beginning to feel a little too old for the endless task of repairing the depredations of our various tenants, clinging to the tops of ladders while painting window frames, working on my knees in the garden, and dealing with a procession of plumbers, electricians, pool men, heating experts, tree men, gas men, TV and radio repair men, rug and curtain cleaners and all the highly paid technicians who are supposed to know how to service refrigerators, dishwashers, clothes washers, dryers and the like, but who sing the constant refrain of "They don't make it like that any more. Better get a new one!"

Now, after sixteen years as a landlord, I have decided to sell out and be a tenant myself if I wish to visit California.

11

George and Benita came out to California in that winter of 1964, and to our astonishment they brought Ted Lowe with them, apparently with the idea of tapping the rich lodes of California gold for their Roturman corporation and its subsidiary Cadco Ltd.

After a few days at the expensive Bel Air Hotel, George went out for a drive one afternoon, in the course of which he bought at sight a luxurious furnished house, complete with swimming pool and garden, in the best section of Beverly Hills.

Even Benita was startled. Ronnie would never have *dreamed* of such a thing! "You know, dear, George is an angel, but he's so impetuous!" she said. However, it wasn't long before a large garden party was thrown for prospective investors.

It seemed that a whole new development of Cadco Ltd. had taken place. The British Board of Trade had refused permission for any further industrial expansion in the county of Sussex, but had offered instead to subsidize Cadco Ltd. and to train its operatives if the company would establish a new factory in the distressed mining area of Glenrothies in Scotland, where there were many unemployed owing to closing of the coal pits. It had been agreed that the company would put up an amount equal to the subsidy, and a loan of £460,000 had been arranged with the Royal Bank of Scotland, which required that the directors should sign a note guaranteeing it. As Lowe and Harris had no money, other than that which they drew from Cadco Ltd., George alone, upon the advice of Lowe, signed it. Elaborate plans were being drawn, and construction was soon to start on the factory and on pens to hold 20,000 pigs.

Now some years before, on my California desert ranch, I had put thirty pigs into existing pens and had soon learned that the care of these cranky animals is a very specialized and difficult business indeed. They suffer from all the infectious diseases that afflict humans, they roll on their young and smother them—and if the young escape they are attacked by foxes and coyotes—and they have other quirks which necessitate constant expert attention. I had been glad to sell them after a few months for a fraction of their value. It was hard to imagine Scottish coal miners coping with them. And there would also be the problem of finding experts capable of superintending the butchering, dressing, packing and sales of the product. I decided to have another private talk with George in the garden, during which I expressed all my fears on these matters.

He thought I was being tiresome and heard me with impatience. "All that is perfectly simple!" he snorted. "We shall just look around for the best men and pay them more than anybody else!"

Benita was so enthralled that I did not dare to express myself to her, but I managed to corner Lowe, from whom I learned that it might be two years before Glenrothies was in operation, and meanwhile the Sussex factory was closed, "to permit the transfer of personnel to Scotland," a prospect which I thought could hardly be attractive to them. Lowe expressed great irritation with Albert Harris, who, he said, was very difficult to work with, being given to long and mysterious absences. In that case, I asked, why not get him out of the company? This was hardly possible, said Lowe, because Albert was a director, and he had recently brought in a woman friend who expected to invest a large amount of capital. This, with unexpected and rapidly mounting costs, was desperately needed.

Shortly after this conversation, Lowe returned to Lausanne. We leased our Santa Monica house and soon followed him. I felt I had done all I could. Benita's enthusiasm for America evaporated even faster than we had expected, for early in the New Year she wrote:

———————

1119 NORTH BEVERLY DRIVE
BEVERLY HILLS

Tuesday

Darlings,

Thank you for your lovely fat letter—you do sound the gay ones, and I can see the Charmettes has started firing on all cylinders with all the rank and fashion pouring in!

You need have no fears that we want to come back here— I for one can't *wait* to be out again, even tho' Dick and Helene arrived last night thank God! I am at least relieved of housework! George is doing a T.V. and did you know they shoot now from 8 a.m. to 7 p.m.? I mean, I ask you!! People are of course falling down in heaps. I think they must be insane. George is naturally *terribly* shocked—you can imagine!— and has vowed never to do another. People we know don't seem to look at it much any more. I think it's on its last legs until Feevee comes in.

After spending a whole day downtown with bankers, investment advisers and lawyers I've come to the conclusion I'll take the Credit Suisse atmosphere of tri-lingual confusion and greed any day in preference to the American Government's barefaced thievery and stupefying taxation. It's just awful, terrifying too because one is never sure where one is going to be attacked next. I came home very stooped and gloomy!

Pat and Joe Cotten have a flop in San Francisco in the Paul Gregory thing, and Kenneth McKenna died, I don't know if you knew him. Ruth Esmond just told me. She knows we don't take these bloody papers, so she calls up every day to give me the mortality tally! Cedric is also quite ill.

Then I spoke to Greer who said she was in great distress because her aunt was seriously ill. So by this time my own spirits had unreasonably rallied and I said "Well you might as well face it, she is probably seriously dying, and since that is something which nature has arranged that you do alone it seems to me essential to achieve some sort of consonance with both life and death, and stop attempting to share the demise of all your elderly relatives, otherwise you are going to have a disproportionately gloomy time for what may be left of your own life."

After a slightly scandalised pause, she replied in a very hearty sort of voice, "I think you're quite right, and we should make a lot of new friends under 30, like Elsie Mendl used to!" I think that is a good idea, except of course new friends are as hard to get along with as old ones are to get along without very often. I guess teething sets the whole pattern: one is always trying to adjust to one set of circumstances or another, although there's been nothing painful about my last set of circumstances. In many ways these last three years have been the happiest in my life with my astonishing friend here!

I really believe the European life is much more agreeable for all of us you know. Countries change so much and there's no doubt America right now is not as attractive as it was 20 years ago. The whole film business is ruled by unionism which is in the process of ruining the entire shebang. It has given tremendous power and absolutely no purpose to the lives of the deeply untalented masses, and all the fun of the creative side, the enthusiasm and general "thrill" of production, has utterly disappeared both for the people who are capable of creating it and the people who used to be vicariously touched by it. Like a bloody coal-mine it is.

Let's retire from everything and have a huge kitchen and a huge studio and a huge workshop and concern ourselves only with artistry, inventions and eating. I don't want to travel or act or go shopping-&-dressing-&-shampooing, I don't want to try to remember my Social Security number, or fill in forms, or consider the charms of my acquaintances in the light of their deductible possibilities, and most of all I don't want to deal with the chronic parking meter, with no change in my bag and a lurking cop waiting to pounce as soon as my time runs out! Life here is a long, losing battle against the invading hordes of restrictions.

Rex Evans has arrived so I will fold my soap box and steal away!

Lots of love

Benita

I think perhaps that at this time Benita, Eleanor and myself were beginning to learn that movement is not necessarily progress, and that happiness is not a place but a state of mind, but these were lessons which George never learned nor wished to learn. Even in the English winter, Benita would have been perfectly happy to live in Kent, if British tax laws had permitted it, but now found herself trapped in California. As for ourselves, after all our years in sunny California, we felt trapped in Lausanne with the discomforts of winter, the brief hours of murky daylight, the dank cold from the Lake, the closed Golf Club, and our friends absent in Marakesh or the Caribbean. For the young and rich, of course, the ski resorts of Switzerland are glorious, but were shrouded in mist to us.

1119 NORTH BEVERLY DRIVE
BEVERLY HILLS

Tuesday

Darlings,

How too maddening about the carpets! We went through just about the same thing. They are all barmy I think. However, one way or another you'll have it all done in about six months so don't let it get you down!

George says that once Jaguars start to go one bolt falls out as you put another in. Come to think of it, we had quite a bit of trouble with mine. The steering died completely on two occasions, so perhaps you should turn yours in. [I am still driving it, twenty years later, despite the total lack of spare parts. —B.A.]

We can't come back *quite* yet but I figure the end of March will do it and then it would be *so* lovely if you could come down to Gibraltar and do a little mousing around with us. Jack Milland was here last night and says he knows of a lovely small house with pool on the coast there for $30,000 which is more the kind of price range one has been looking for, so we feel quite encouraged. Vinnie and Mary Price were here too. I suppose you heard she is pregnant. Isn't it a riot?

That Jack Paar show is *extraordinary*. It baffles me how people can watch it, *riddled* with sponsor spots which give it all the charm of a bad case of smallpox and two hours of bad-libbing in the middle of the night. I should have thought it the kind of exposure you can die of—but not at all! On the contrary, Henry Morgan is doing almost exactly the same thing, as if one wasn't enough!

I'm not at all surprised that Kit Cornell has never seen George act. Judging by some of her performances which I have caught, I would think there are strong grounds for doubt that she even sees her vis-à-vis. I think she is a chronic drunk for great, heady draughts of foaming Cornell which have clouded her vision to the point where the rest of the world is barely discernible.

Juliet is in Paris supposedly to take advantage of all the intoxicating culture that France has to offer, instead of which I have the clear and dispiriting impression that, drunk with freedom, she is boning up heavily on American movies! Not at all what one had in mind, dreaming of her carrying on in three languages with a galaxy of Ambassadors while buttoning her gloves. It would be nice if she even got as far as *having* a button on her gloves—or anything else for that matter!

You did make us giggle about Martha! She really is a crashing bore, and always looks so *drained*, doesn't she. She rather reminds me of Winnie Baxter, great ox of a dame who can't do a hands turn of anything. I'm sure if she had to make the beds she'd faint dead away! Maybe she'll cheer up when they get into the Lowe Rivage—and brother, will *that* ever be a project to get furnished!

Lots of love from us both

Benita

Friday

Darlings,

We are due to arrive March 8th and I see you are leaving March 7th which is about par for the course. Anyhow you are coming back in a few days aren't you? And is Ellie going too or will she be over for dinner Thursday and get all the news in first? Don't go to Rome by car for God's sake—it won't be at all a nice drive this time of the year, so fly down and come right back and stay in Lausanne till we have to go again around the 24th. Then you can be in Italy in April which is a much nicer month, things beginning to green up a bit and blossoms and all that. Then England at the end of May for all of us. After that we are going to go and look for our Spanish palazzo—only now you have dragged a great *boat* into the scene which has got us terribly unsettled!

Ah, but I would dearly love to have a roomy sort of a house, the kind about which you *don't* say "It has a beautifully *arranged* kitchen—you see one doesn't want a great *big* one." Well I do! I want a *big* kitchen and a *big* bedroom and a *big* bathroom—all on a *big* estate which goes on for miles and miles at $50 an acre! I'm sick of these ingenious modern houses where every inch counts and there's barely room for thought. If I stand in my bathroom here with my arms akimbo I have to forgo breathing. There's definitely not room for both, so you have a straight choice. Not that I'm so devoted to standing with my arms akimbo: actually it is the word rather than the position that appeals to me.

I suppose you couldn't go to Rome a few days earlier by any chance? Maybe? No harm in asking? Ellie, you *can't* go too anyway. As George says, "You *have* to come over right away!" We are longing to see you.

Lots of love.

Benita

12

Now all our plans were abruptly changed. Eleanor and Benita began to complain that they didn't know where their roots were, but the life of the wife of a working expatriate actor is not an easy one. George sold the Beverly Hills house as impetuously as he had bought it, and I received an offer to make a picture in Yugoslavia for an American company. We flew to Rome for preproduction discussions, costume fittings and so on.

It seemed that Martin Melcher, the husband of Doris Day, had made a handsome profit from the exhibition of her pictures abroad and sought a way of repatriating it, or secreting it, without attracting the attention of the U.S. Internal Revenue Service—no easy trick. He bought a good script, *The Cavern*, written by one of the famous "Hollywood Ten" Communist sympathizers who had been disbarred from the screen but still wrote, when occasion offered, under assumed names. This story concerned a small group of soldiers of various nationalities, both friend and foe, who took refuge from a bombing attack in a chain of mountain caves and found themselves sealed in together when an unlucky bomb shut the entrance.

My part was very good, I thought, both amusing and touching, being that of an old-style British Army Colonel. As director, we had Edgar Ulmer, a rather florid, temperamental character who had much experience and some talent but so far not much success. He and Melcher had visited the gigantic and famous caves at Postojna, high in the Yugoslavian mountains behind Trieste, and had quickly decided they would make an ideal location for the story. The Yugoslavs had promised every cooperation, and Melcher had flown back to Hollywood, leaving poor Ulmer with total responsibility for everything and—as we were to find later—barely half the money necessary to shoot the picture.

Ulmer and his loyal, overworked wife, who acted as assistant producer, script girl, wardrobe mistress, secretary, cashier and everything else necessary, plunged into their tasks and scarcely slept for many weeks. I was totally unaware of these circumstances, of course, being accustomed to the order and superb organization of the great Hollywood Studios, where my contractual matters were always handled by my agent, to whom in this case a contract had been sent and was forwarded to me for signature. I was rather surprised to see that it had been signed not by Melcher but by Ulmer, on behalf of a company registered in Liberia! I was given a date on which to report at Postojna, but nothing was said about the cost of my transportation there or about my fares and hotel expenses on the trip to Rome, but I assumed that all that would be adjusted later.

We returned to Lausanne to find the Sanderses had left for England and also that, as Benita had predicted, the steering mechanism of my Jaguar had broken down and it was necessary to order a new pump from the factory in England. This arrived just twenty-four hours before we were due in Postojna, was hastily installed, and we left in the night in order to reach our destination the following evening. As we at last crossed the frontier and climbed the bleak mountains, we found them covered in snow. On our arrival, exhausted and starving, we found the only building was a small, bare tourist hotel, recently built of wood to house the summer visitors who come to visit the caves, and in this were crammed the cast, including Peter Marshall, later famous as the M.C. of the television show *Hollywood Squares*; Larry Hagman, the son of Mary Martin; and John Saxon—all of whom have since made their mark, and also an entire Italian crew. The discomfort was appalling, the rooms tiny, the food uneatable, and the outlook dreary beyond words. I need hardly add that the morale of the whole company had already sunk *very* low.

For a few days, we shot exteriors on the mountains, in the freezing, paralyzing cold, drinking Yugoslavian brandy out of the bottle to keep alive and trying to communicate in several languages. We were then informed that shooting must be abandoned on that location because the caves, which I never saw, were closed in winter, being filled with ice and cut off from any electricity for light, heat or power! Apparently the hotel normally closed too with the coming of autumn. The whole company with all its equipment was moved down to Trieste, where imitation caves were hastily built in the local swimming baths. I say hastily, but actually it turned out to be a case of "the more haste, the less speed," because the local workmen had never seen a movie company at work and had no idea where to start. Trieste, which had been the great port of the Austro-Hungarian Empire, had been seized by the Italians at the end of World War I, but it had proved to be too remote to be useful to them and had dwindled into a picturesque but poor town. It was there that we heard of the assassination of Kennedy, and the world seemed to be coming to an end. Eleanor and I took advantage of the delays to spend a few lovely days in Venice.

THE DORCHESTER
PARK LANE, LONDON

Wednesday

Darlings,

We keep getting indignant letters from you saying you never hear from us and we *never* know where you are! One day I sat down and telephoned Postojna, Trieste and Rome successively and the upshot was that the Excelsior told us to try the Wm. Morris Agency! At last we have—or rather I have, because George is at the Studio where he is doing a very funny film with Peter Sellers—the full, frightful story of your comings and goings, and it is really too awful. I just hope you are not stuck in the caves of Postojna too long—we were trying madly to get hold of you to say "Make for the border and to hell with them!" I tell you, after eight weeks in Budapest I know how you feel. We were absolutely frantic, and became hysterical when we reached Vienna and walked into the royal suite at the Imperial decorated in scarlet and gold and with about five acres of chandeliers on the ceilings, fruit, flowers, champagne, hey nonny nonny and hoopla! We couldn't believe it was true as we had become convinced we were going to be staggering around in the great, grey, greasy Limpopo of communism for the rest of our lives. It beats me how people can either want it or stand it. All that following and spying and microphoning, and fear —a hopeless, helpless, pointless, paintless kind of life. Ugh!

I sympathise with your lack of interest in the caves. I would go further and say that nothing would persuade me to go into one. Juliet insisted on going into a grotto thing in Rapallo and I would have screamed the place down if I hadn't been frightened of it resulting in just that!

It's so lovely being back in London. George is always going on about "contrast," and maybe he's right for it seems like paradise, pure paradise, and it's not often one says that about November in England!

Lots of love

Benita

Our next move was to some ancient abandoned caves outside Rome, again freezing cold and ankle deep in sticky mud, to which I was driven in darkness and drizzling rain daily, eating horrid lunches of cold pasta out of cardboard boxes while sitting on the ground. Every few days it seemed the money gave out and somebody went on strike, the electricians, the camera crew or the actors—including myself, I am ashamed to say, because I hated to add to the poor Ulmers' problems which reduced them, and indeed all of us, to despair, but I was not getting paid.

We had taken an apartment, sight unseen, in Rome and on our arrival, after a long drive from Trieste, we found it so gloomy that Eleanor declared she could not be left alone in it while I was working. Frantic phone calls produced a friend who agreed to rent her nice but expensive penthouse to us, so then we had two apartments, until at long last the picture dragged to some sort of an end. Eleanor and I drove back to Lausanne, disenchanted with the European film industry but thankful to be alive.

SHEPPERTON STUDIOS
MIDDLESEX

March 1964

Dear Brian,

Though sometimes hard to believe, pictures have a way of coming to an end. The picture you are making now is no exception to the rule; it WILL come to an end. YOU WILL WIN THROUGH TO FREEDOM. Furthermore, a wonderful compensation awaits you once it's over: as a result of what we went through in Budapest, the "delightful Miss Hume" —as Roderick Mann calls her—and I are enjoying London as we never have before. The contrast is marvellous. I personally am also enjoying for the first time in my life making a movie, for the same reason.

We are all much too spoiled, and tend to spoil ourselves more and more. A rough experience, such as you are having now, will pay marvellous dividends when it is over. So have courage and concentrate on the light at the end of the tunnel; it will grow bigger and brighter every day.

George

While in Rome, we had been taken to a large cocktail party which was being given, we were told, by the sausage king from England, who was reputed to throw the most lavish parties in town. As I stood in the crush, glass in hand, some-

137

one said to me, "Brian, let me introduce you to our host, Mr. Albert Harris."

I turned and saw a plump young man, with hand outstretched, whose appearance so shocked me that I took an involuntary step backward! Was this phoney, smirking rascal the man upon whom our friends had staked their fortunes? I could not believe it. My heart sank as I stood staring at him, but I quickly recovered and we exchanged a few pleasantries about George and Benita. I then asked him what he was doing in Rome. "Tying up the Italian fruit industry," he replied cheerfully, and went on to tell me that he was also promoting a motion picture, to be called *Give My Love a Gun*, and that when that production was finished and sold he would be going to the Argentine.

"The Argentine!" I said in astonishment. "What for?"

"To tie up the beef industry!" he replied, and with that he turned and invited the twenty remaining people to dinner at an expensive restaurant. Limousines were provided and we all spent a gay and costly evening, without doubt paid for by the luckless investors in Cadco Ltd.

I wrote a cautious letter to Benita, hinting rather than expressing my alarm. I was not sure if she knew about the Husan scandal in California and I was careful not to imply any criticism of George, but I told her of our meeting with Harris and of the bad impression he had made on us.

THE DORCHESTER
PARK LANE, LONDON

Sunday

Darling hearts,

You seem to have had an average encounter with Al. He is quite astonishing, and I am sure if you were stone deaf in both ears he would still be able to leave you in a very advanced state of stupefaction after half an hour! Well you know the Rome thing is in aid of the Cadco factories going up in Italy, with which project I imagine Al has already regaled you. George refers to it as a fait accompli but I haven't really given it my full attention as actually I am not quite unpacked at Weeks yet! Perhaps we shall be in Rome. I shan't be surprised. Unprepared as usual, but unsurprised is what I shall be.

I left this open because I had a suspicion I would have more to tell you on that subject, and I have! It now looks as if we were going to live in Rome after George and Al's last conversation—from which, incidentally, George emerged in such a euphoric state of self-aggrandisement that he was mortally offended to discover that he couldn't have the Harlequin Suite here for two months! I managed to conceal my disappointment but one thing is clear: if Al really pulls it all off George will have no trouble in getting rid of the dough! Of course I can't honestly say that it is a problem of mine either, but I'm always impressed by George's unconfined and disdainful grandeur! He already has people looking for the most gilded palazzo in Rome where we can entertain villainous Italian business men and shifty ministers in marbled splendour!

We saw the most gilded and glorious production of *Boheme* in Vienna and also a charming Strauss in what looked like an old and beautiful ballroom—but the others, *Flying Dutchman* —honestly! That ghastly first act! We didn't stay for the rest —and *Carmen* and a ballet were all very poor and we didn't sit through any of them, but isn't it a smashing opera house? All those hundreds of chandeliers! Absolute heaven.

I see Sylvia all the time. She has just had a *desk* stolen which I think is very outlandish. It was sent to an auctioneer to be sold, and being a signed French piece and priced at £6000 it was put carefully in the warehouse from which it was equally carefully removed. Furthermore it was somehow done when there was no insurance on it! We were discussing this at the Tooth Gallery in Brook St. but they were already full of self-pity, having had a Renoir stolen *off the wall* the previous day! As the saying goes, "I don't know what we are coming to!" And then the appalling disaster of Kennedy's assassination. London is swaddled in half-masted flags. I never saw anything like it before. I shall post this and George can write a separate one to fatten your mail as I know so well

139

how much it means in those dreary circumstances. We *can't* go on working in these mad locations.

Lots of love darlings.

Benita

SHEPPERTON STUDIOS
MIDDLESEX

December 1964

Dear Brian

I think the time has come for an agonizing reappraisal of our situation. The fact is that the Swiss gimmick with the Roturman contract only makes sense for people with a high earning power in the international film-making business. For people whose earning power is relatively modest, it just does not make any sense at all to sit around in a country which has a lousy climate, where one has to struggle with the language in the sense that one can never hope to master it and dominate it and enjoy its subtle uses; a country whose authorities conceal behind a pretence of hospitality a nauseating condescension to the moneyed foreigner and dangle before him their lousy "Permis de séjour" as if it were some priceless gift from heaven. We have given it a fair trial, but "Mene Mene Tekel Upharsin."

And so, some time in April, we shall pull out of England and go to Rome, where we shall settle down and I shall become "Cadco's Man in Rome." If we are successful in this venture, then Rome will become our permanent base. As an executive of Cadco Italia (a company operating at the invitation of the Italian Government), I shall have no personal income tax liability, and consequently will have no need to maintain a residence in Switzerland. I think it is high time you seriously considered entering upon a sensible, dignified business career, instead of perpetuating the puerile follies of an adolescent thespian, and I shortly telephone you with a most interesting suggestion.

Love

George

This letter of course delighted me, for it was real vintage Sanders, written with authority and a fine command of the English language, almost every sentence a challenge to common sense. The "lousy" Swiss Permis de Séjour against which he inveighs is no more than the American Resident Alien green card with which he had lived for years. "Cadco Italia" was an obvious fraud, based upon the conception that everything is fraudulent in Italy and developed with no mention or thought of the enormous undertaking in Scotland, of which he was the sole guarantor. "The puerile follies of an adolescent thespian" had been, and still were, the only source of all the money he had poured down so many drains in his endless search for the pot of gold at the foot of some imaginary rainbow. I had once written to him, "Relax! You have found it in Benita," and I was not going to incur hostility by writing it again, but I must confess I awaited the promised phone call with lively curiosity.

WEEKS FARM
EGERTON
KENT

Christmas Day

Darling hearts,
Thank you Ellie for your lovely fat under-the-dryer letter. I suppose there can't be too much to choose between one cave and another cave, but I refuse to feel sorry for Brian coming home to one or other of your Roman apartments! Honestly! I never heard of anything as high class as you two!

George's mother and mine have come to visit—there'll be a hot time in the old town tonight—and I have just left them with the T.V. which has supplanted all former means of communication and really makes much social effort superfluous. Well to be candid *any* social or conversational moves—outside of slipping a drink silently into the hand—are apt to be received with thinly disguised hostility if delivered in the course of the ten hours during which the machine is in action. Actually this takes a lot of the onus off prolonged domestic encounters, although that is probably not the result all those dedicated actors had in mind.

I don't think we'll meet in Rome you know because we'll go to Lausanne about Feb 7th, which should be when you go? Then we're planning to go to Rome in March if our industrial empire doesn't crumble in its Italian phase. We should know about that around Jan 20th. Al was here yesterday and says he knows of a grand apartment on top of that red building on the left of the Fountain of Trevi which I think sounds great. Do you know it? I always figure you know everybody and everything that's cooking around town!

If by any chance you should be on your way here, one never knows, I need hardly say that Weeks is open to, in fact downright gasping for your custom. Then we can all go house-hunting in London for Ellie's roots. I know exactly what she means because since I have been in orbit with George I feel like that picture of Alice hurtling along in the Red Queen's grip while she shouts "In our country you have to run as fast as you can just to stay in the same place!"

Lots of love

Benita

p.s. George just called up from the Studio and made me read your letter on the telephone so he wouldn't have to wait till tonight!

THE DORCHESTER
PARK LANE, LONDON

Tuesday

Oh, I just found your postcard Ellie! That was a very crafty manoeuvre going to Venice—I would *adore* a palazzo there, although I'm inclined to think the season has become almost insupportable with the tourists. Perhaps we could have a lovely *little*-off-season in the *early* summer, but mind you this does nothing to solve our root problem; it's just getting carried away by one more crazy place!

We went over and lunched with Viv Leigh and Jack the other day and then brought them back to Weeks for dinner which was fun. She is looking glorious and Jack is very nice, but Viv still talks mostly of Larry and I think torments herself and is sad.

I had a funny letter from Noël who is still complaining bitterly that George wouldn't play *The Sleeping Prince*. "I have always been quite fond of him," he wrote, "but I didn't think I would go to the theatre every night and *yearn* for him." He went on to say Jose Ferrer's voice leaves practically everything to be desired and added crossly, "I suppose *you* thought he played Toulouse Lautrec on his knees. Untrue. He was standing bolt upright!" So I think we may take it he is not very happy.

I haven't seen any theatre here. Should see *Uncle Vanya* I suppose but it's a rather dispiriting prospect.

Oh dear, I *wish* you would come out of your cave. Can't imagine how they ever figured on getting enough light in the first place. Barmy, that's what.

Benita

Suddenly George's promised call came. He offered me the job of Special Public Relations Representative for Cadco Italia in Rome!

"Why me?" I gasped in astonishment. "I know nothing about such things!"

"You don't have to know anything," he answered impatiently. "You and Eleanor are very good with people, and giving swanky dinners, and all that. All you have to do is to entertain the right Italian officials and pass them money under the table!"

I declined this amazing offer with thanks. Not only did I feel totally unsuited to such a task, but I was horrified about the future of a company which had such an enormous investment in Glenrothies, Scotland, not to mention the investments of the Royal Bank of Scotland and the British Government, and whose three directors had apparently been devoting their time, one to his law practice in Lausanne, another to his workshop in Kent, and the third to tying up the Italian and Argentine fruit and beef industries, while at the same time pouring the parent company's money down the rathole of the Italian movie business.

They did not go to Rome in April, but wrote that they were off to the Bahamas instead. I called at once and pointed out to George that they had invested all their money in the Cadco venture in Scotland. It seemed to me, I said, that from what I had heard in Rome it was vital that, if they went anywhere, it should be to Glenrothies. How, I asked him, did he hope to run the company from the Bahamas?

"Really, old man, what nonsense you do talk!" he exclaimed. "I can have a directors' meeting in Nassau, can't I?"

I replied that if I had such a responsibility I was damn sure I couldn't, and this seemed to annoy him. Benita, he said, had been suffering from mysterious pains which had been diagnosed in London as acute arthritis, and the doctors insisted that she must live in a hot climate. A Bahamian real estate development company—probably in the mistaken belief that George had large funds available for investment—had offered him gratis a fine piece of property at Freeport, on which they could build a home outside the British tax area, which of course appealed to George, and this they were going to look at. Off they went, only to find that it was one of hundreds of small unsold squares of waterless sandy ground, with no vegetation and inhabited only by myriads of sandflies and scuttling land crabs, very different from the luxury to which they were accustomed! They left at once for New York, and as usual by the time they got back to Europe we had left for California.

CHEMIN DE MONTOLIVET 27
LAUSANNE

Darlings,

We spent a few days in New York. Of course it was freezing and I arrived as always superbly equipped in seven cotton shifts and a borrowed mink which was none the less welcome for trailing tastefully around my ankles. However, we had a very interesting time and George and Ted are going back soon for two days—I am trying to persuade myself to stay behind—to talk about a deal which might make us all very light-hearted and heavily-heeled. Well, there's always something on George's hob as you know.

California sounds *divine* from your lyrical description. To add to your pleasure I must tell you it is cold and wet here. We went to visit the Krasnas in their new palazzo which is really marvellously comfortable and I think a great piece of luck to have fallen upon. [Fallen upon? We found it for them. —B.A.] George of course fixed their bedroom lights for them and I covered the switch in mink! The next day we received a large can of caviar and some vodka with a card saying "Don't feel flattered. We give this to all the help." He's a funny man I do think.

The Holdens came to dinner *together!* Imagine! Bill looked very much improved and has forsworn both the demon rum and Capucine—or so the rumour goes. He is still living in the apartment however and only occasionally addresses a remark to Ardis, and then looks rather startled as if he were astonished to find her in the room. She sits dove-grey and silent and wringing her hands. She says though that she feels optimistic that they will live happily ever after one day: on what she bases this wild surmise is not immediately apparent.

It's miserable here without you both. The Chaplins are away too in Ireland and the Whitneys not back yet. Those confounded Shereks are all over the place though.

Ted says he is going to have a Bank! I thought of "wild thyme," or perhaps even "time." But it is all very big stuff. Can't say he is a stick-in-the-mud, can we?

I bet you are adoring working about your lovely house and pool and all. I tell you, these apartments get very claustrophobic after a while. I must go to bed.

Benita

Darlings,

I haven't answered your lovely letters because I have been layed supine for five weeks by lumbago! And I want to tell you that I can think of things that I would rather be. Layed supine that is. It was agony; I could hardly turn over in bed, and I tried all sorts of cures. The Swiss, rather uncharacteristically, have a strong fancy for quacks and I had, from a society-type doctor, pins stuck *all* over me on the grounds that the Chinese cured *everything* that way, a theory which struck no spark of confidence in me, and had no results either, other than my strong feeling of indignation. In the end I came to an agreement with the doctor (who was divine, very chic and merry) that we would visit each other socially but with no medical intent, which has worked very well as he has a nice chalet and a gay mistress and we all enjoyed it! Then I went to a mysterious man who I think cures chickens of the bends and that type of thing. He was very civil and ushered me into his *dining* room, which sort of made a change, and after giving me a few ugly shoves pronounced me cured in ringing tones which bore no relation to the facts. That's all that happened there. Then I took Dr Sanders' cure of fasting. For almost three days I lay in bed quite still, because I was in pain, and Dr Sanders lay beside me because he was asleep, and at the end of it I was a good deal thinner but still had lumbago! Well anyhow it's better now.

George has started on his film and calls me at short intervals to explain the intolerable burdens of being an actor, but as I saw him tooling off towards the Ritz in his beautiful Roly-Poly, dressed in a pale grey triumph of Mr Tromble's, it seemed to me he was managing to hold his own in this hard world.

I don't think Joe Cotten and Pat Medina will really tie up, do you? anyhow they are both darlings and I hope they are enjoying themselves. Pat must be a Godsend for Joe to have around, so pretty and warm and gay and funny and everything. I spoke to Deb Kerr when they were spliced and she sounded madly happy; they have built a Disneyland house she said, up there in Klosters, and were obviously awash with silver linings which was nice. Peter is a very amusing interesting sort of fellow—much nicer than Tony, who is really awfully thickheaded I think, don't you? I think the Swiss real estate situation is grotesque, and what's more I don't think it's a good investment at these insane prices. They simply can't go up further unless by raging inflation.

How was Viv? Do give her my love. I think about her often and I *do* hope she doesn't wither away. She is such a terrific creature I am sure all sorts of splendid things will happen for her if she can get rid of this obsession about Larry. Incidentally we haven't seen Larry yet and I am still having trouble walking so haven't been to London but I expect I'll nip up this week—all the divorcées are there—Jimmy Granger and Michael Wilding as well—all having the most fatuous reports in the press about "keeping it all from the children" and the usual tripe.

George has been tearing round the country on his motor bike with Juliet on the back. When I say "tearing" it doesn't really give an accurate picture of his progress since Juliet told me she had to get off and push every time they encountered a slight incline, and G. always goes so slowly that the machine balks at the least hazard. We were once overtaken by a dachshund when I was riding with him!

He really is the best natured creature and I do hope I am not becoming maudlin about him, although I sometimes suspect that my attitude of cool irony has suffered some changes which are not entirely concealed. We want to come over to California for Christmas. I wonder if I could manage it, that would really be nice. Well, we'll see.

Lots of love to you both,

Benita

RITZ HOTEL
LONDON W.1

Monday

Darlings,

Your *harping* on the sunshine has had its effect on our sodden imaginations and we are coming out for three weeks over Christmas, probably about Dec 22nd, but rather depending on what day Sarah Bernhardt Colman gets out of school. So what are you doing Christmas night? We're going to the Beverly Hills Hotel unless someone is leaving town and will rent us their house—this isn't a hint as, like yourself, I wouldn't stay with anyone for more than three days. [Referring to an Italian saying which I am apt to quote: "L'ospite, come il pesce, dopo tre giorni, puzza!" Guests, like fish, after three days stink! —B.A.]

I must tell you that England isn't really an island any longer, just a heavily populated part of the sea. Honestly, this year the whole bloody thing is practically submerged.

Isn't it fine about Pat and Joe Cotten? I hope all goes well for them. Glynis Johns is taking the big step this week too, with a nice man who has been padding around her for some time.

We take off for Turkey next week for a film. This makes for great one-upmanship in conversation but what it is actually like I have no idea. Anyway we shall be there for two weeks, back here for two weeks and then back to Lausanne until we come to America. It will be divine to see you both again and I hope you are not going away or anything awful like that? Have you got over the hump with your autobiography?

Ellie, for God's sake get your crochet instructions together for me; I have been having a ghastly time trying to figure out my mauve shawl you gave me which I want to copy! Lots of love.

Benita

We heard no more about the picture in Turkey, so we must assume either that it was canceled or that George "discarded" it. He went through a period of advocating that as a solution to life's problems. I can remember walking down Fifth Avenue in New York with him and saying that I must go into Saks to buy a pair of shoes. I said I had many pairs of old shoes but got bored with wearing them and then didn't know what to do with them.

"Discard them!" said George. "One should discard anything that bores one." Then he chuckled and nudged me. "I'll tell you something else," he said. "One can discard friends too!"

"Maybe, George," I replied, "but not you. After all, you only have two, Stewpot and myself, and if you discard one of us you will only have one left, won't you?"

He took no offense at this. On the contrary, he seemed to enjoy it.

MONTOLIVET 27
LAUSANNE

Tuesday

Darlings,

Loved your letter and enclosures and are of course *delighted* to hear you will be around when we're out there. I *hated* seeing your tenants in residence last time—it looked all *wrong!*

Pat and Joe arrive on Thursday to stay with the Nivens so I hope we shall see them. I also hear that Hedda Hopper arrived at Montreux for a stay, and *that* makes us settlers restless in the hills tonight! You can bet she's out to cook up some ghastly article about the Alpine Set! Well I hope the old bitch falls in the Lake.

Noël tells me Viv and Merivale are coming to stay soon too. I think she's going to make a picture in Rome or something. He brought Lionel Bart over the other night, the man who has written the big musical hit *Oliver*. He's like Irving Berlin, only he *really* can't play, even in C. I think it's so amazing to have, as it were, a hit in the head. Looks like Irving too, which is not so good!

This talk about temperatures over 90 drives us mad. It's pouring again today. Bloody awful climate and we are white-skinned and fat like steamed turbots. We'll keep you informed about our very erratic movements but I think we'll be out around the 20th. Ellie, *do* come to Robinsons with me —I do so hate shopping with George, who keeps saying "Well, what are you *looking* for?" I wouldn't mind so much but the silly man expects an *answer!* I got the most divine little 18th Century table, the kind that has two legs and goes on the wall—can't remember what they are called—which I had seen when I was mousing around months ago, and it proves how "just looking" pays off, it's between the windows in the dining room with two golden candelabra on it and it looks a treat.

Much love

Benita

MONTOLIVET 27
LAUSANNE

Darlings,

In case you are interested, Hedda Hopper is at Dr Niehans' Clinic, hoping no doubt for rejuvenation. *I* think he is an almighty phoney who bases his reputation on the astounding premise that he *cured the Pope's hiccups!* You know one wouldn't dare to use such a circumstance as a dramatic device! I mean one cannot even see the Pope *having* hiccups, so unpractical with all that towering hardware he has on his head. Then the Vatican censor would surely not pass such a blasphemous libel on God's Vicar's digestion. And to top it off he comes trooping over to Niehans who applies his usual over-all prescription of denying all food for a couple of days, whereupon the Pope was cured in the first ten minutes. Of the hiccups that is. He died not long after, a side effect no doubt which seems to have escaped the general observation. One hopes nobody was indiscreet enough to put "Hic" Jacet Popus Bonus on his tombstone.

I must admit Bob Cummings looks mortifyingly well, but I always understood that was due to a lifetime denial of all the things that make life tolerable—drink and such—and I'm not sure that I don't prefer to die from a surfeit of life than to live looking, and for all one knows feeling, like a crocodile handbag which, after all, is Somerset Maugham's situation.

Your letter was sensational. What a marvellous expression, the "stately gaiety" of our correspondence! I wish I had thought of that!

The London newspaper which published Zsa Zsa's memoirs "very graciously" sent the proofs to George in case he wanted anything deleted. G. began to read them and bogged down, then I took over and bogged down too, so that was it as far as we went. I did not think Gerold Frank was up to her at all, but then I didn't read much.

As for George's recondite virtues, he is like the rest of us; if he has got what he wants, and his vis-à-vis wants what he's got, he's an angel. Manifestly not a saint—whose exalted position, when all is said and done, depends mainly on surviving other people's vices—but definitely an angel, compassionate, imperturbably good-humoured, gay, the sprightliest mind imaginable, "unto himself true," without guile and anyhow, as far as I am concerned, a man to make every day one to which I look forward with joy. Ah well, perhaps I was born with rose-coloured eyeballs! I don't see why Larry is doing your piece. I rather took umbrage. I do hope Ellie that your aunt has not taken roots: your houses darling are entirely too beguiling: one risotto and people are there for life!

The Nivens have taken the plunge and bought the Château d'Oex Chalet. It is very nice and comfortable and right on top of the ski lift which they adore so I think it very wise of them.

How awful about Clark. That poor Kay. What an unbearable shock and loss. One wonders how she will survive, with the baby yet to come and her own heart troubles.

Merle and Bruno were here and in great form. Merle absolutely smashing in a great dripping sable coat—not jacket, *coat!*—and pearls the size of chrysanthemums, and her diamond ring on which you could float a swan in need of exercise! What a dame she is! We are going there for Christmas lunch—where the hell will you be?

Oh dear! Oh dear! Your back! I shall come charged with European drugs, like Butazolidine on which I am now an expert, to cure your ills. Lots of love from both.

Benita

They did not come to California that Christmas. Benita was too ill to stand the trip. They went instead to London to consult a Harley Street specialist, who confirmed the Swiss diagnosis of arthritis and recommended a course of hot radioactive mud baths at Abano in Italy. They flew there from London.

GRAND HOTEL ROYAL OROLOGIO
ABANO

Monday

We bloody nearly lost the plane, what with George losing his way and the frightul pandemonium at Thief Row, as they call it now. We had booked a double room with a *balcony* as a concession to luxury. However the manager had other plans and having given us a royal welcome explained that he perfectly understood how unsuitable it would be for me to take the treatment in the general department and consequently was happy to show us a suite with its own private room for the mud, which you have put on as you recline on a massage table amid beautifully tiled walls and a bath you walk down into and sit there in irradiated (or something) water. Our sitting room has slate blue curtains and walls, chandeliers and a splendid bunch of carnations which, with two bottles of perfume, come from the triumphant management. And just to think, one used to keep well by walking the dog! Still, I think you'll have to try it.

First the doctor comes in, and to say he is ebullient is like saying Niagara is dripping. His conversation is conducted in four languages and his opening gambit is to burst through the door shouting "Is anyone alive?" in several of them. "You speak Russian like a Pole—and Italian like a Russian," he cried to George in French, and by the time he's through taking your blood pressure you feel you've finished the last act of *Cosi Fan Tutti*. It's all terribly exciting, or would be if I didn't feel so awful.

Only the Chaplins were home when we left Lausanne so we dined together at St Saphorin which I enjoyed but George says he finds Charlie too phoney which results as we all know in G. being as chatty as a rock. I like him though. Charlie I mean. Well, George too for that matter!

We hear that Noël has returned from Jamaica with a new *local* boy friend. Ted Lowe told George that Noël brought him to dinner where he took the opportunity of remarking to Martha that he had discovered a sore spot on his Peter (sic) which the doctor subsequently diagnosed as syphilis! Most unfortunately I was not present (I still can't bring myself to hob nob with Ted) so I don't know whether Martha was carried out or what the upshot of this outrageous bit of reminiscence was. Can you imagine such staggering behaviour? Although I must admit there is something faintly endearing about selecting Martha as his confidante in such a matter!

Well, George has now gone to Rome for a meeting with Albert, and if this Cadco Italia thing goes through I suppose we shall be packing up and leaving Lausanne, and I don't know how I can face it. Oh dear me, we are living in a turmoil. I *shall* be glad if and when we find a house again of our *own;* right now I feel suspended like that woman in the magic trick who lies in mid-air and has a loop passed over her. For God's sake write me. Despond is what I am in the slough of. Oh dear me how trying it all is.

13

And now came a thunderclap.

MONTOLIVET 27
LAUSANNE

16th January 1965

Dear Brian,

Yesterday morning at 9 o'clock, at the Clinique Cecile, Ave Ruchonnet, Lausanne, Benita underwent an emergency operation for cancer of the chest.

She survived it well, and is making normal progress towards recovery.

Juliet and I visited her later in the day, and found her in good heart.

Juliet's bosom school friend, a snotty little girl called Mouse, had chosen the same day to elope with an Arab boy-friend. They got married, illegally (she is under-age), and are off, despite her mother's tears and supplications, to the black tents of Saudi Arabia.

Juliet herself was so upset by this news that when we visited Benita she could talk of nothing else, and I couldn't help feeling, although I understand very little of such matters, that in the presence of a woman who was fighting for her life, the conversation was of doubtful therapeutic value.

However, Benita treated the matter with tolerant amusement, there being no axe handy.

OTHER NEWS IN BRIEF

1. We all got a big bang out of your letter. Especially the bit about New York enjoying Freedom from the Press—Very witty!—You should be on the Telly!

2. Billie will probably come to Lausanne at the end of this month to do the cooking during Benita's convalescence as we are losing Dick and Helene.

3. Billie's arrival will be the signal for my departure. I will go to England to make a picture so that she can have my bed.

4. The Rolls Royce is still in my possession. Jack Cardiff couldn't raise the money. We are now up to our ass in motor cars.

5. Benita's room-mate (sic) is King Ibn Saud. He and his twenty wives are occupying all the rooms that have bathrooms, even though they don't know what bathrooms are for. Poor Benita has to make do with a commode. I understand from the nurses that the King has the clap.

Love

George

CLINIQUE CECILE
LAUSANNE

Benita

Darlings,

I know George has told you my grizzly news because he read me one of his letters which I am sure made you laugh as much as it did me. He's a remarkable man all right, and never more so than now. I don't think he casts any shade, all you have to do is stick around and he just shines all over you. It's all true about Ibn Saud being here. He's taken the *whole floor* above this. Travelling light though, only has 12 wives with him. However, even such austerity leaves one wondering quite how they fit their particular function into a hospital routine, not that they are in any close connection with a hospital routine. Last night, towards 3 a.m., they got to singing him some *very* long songs—nothing from the Top Ten I would say.

I'm sure I'm going to die, but the doctor and George say this is not so and indeed I'm supposed to be out of here at the end of the week, albeit not so fully abreast of the situation as when I came in. I've had a perfectly horrific experience, I'm sure the worst thing since the unveiling of the Mona Lisa which I hear was exceedingly trying too.

Huge snowflakes are drifting about outside in a lethargic, disorderly sort of way, as if they had only the sketchiest notion of which way was down, and the seagulls come beautifully and eat bread on my balcony. The nurses are so sweet; I think one of them lives inside a walnut, in fact I'm rather tending toward the view that she *is* a walnut. As George says, she talks to me as if I were a little cat, and I become exceedingly pitiful the moment she appears.

Loved your letters. That Basil!!! *Honestly!* Come back soon.

Lots of love.

Benita

She wrote to her friend Lilli Palmer that she was visiting a doctor in Lausanne for an ordinary checkup when he fairly brutally told her that she had cancer in both breasts which should be removed immediately. She sat stunned, at first unable to believe it and then, pleading for a different verdict, she asked if he was absolutely certain, was there no other way, no form of treatment possible ? The doctor, she wrote, was a brute who had neither time. nor patience for her and was, in fact, rather annoyed by her questions.

"You ought to be glad to be alive afterwards," he barked. Don't be so vain! You're afraid for your décolleté, that's the long and the short of it!" With that, he dismissed her and she stumbled home on foot through the snow and sleet, hardly knowing where she was going.

George was at home and without taking off her coat she went to him and collapsed in tears in his arms. He was very alarmed and asked what in God's name had happened, but for a moment she was unable to talk coherently. She finally blurted out that both her breasts would have to be removed. The dreadful man heaved a sigh of relief as he said, "Oh, is that all? Well, who needs them?"

The next scene plays on the day she dreaded. After leaving the hospital where she had been duly instructed, she went to a certain address which catered for women in her particular trouble as well as for flat-chested girls. The saleswoman was not at all sympathetic or concerned as she led Benita to a curtained-off cubicle. "We're having a busy day today," she announced briskly. "You're the fifth client this morning, Modom."

Benita was glad of her businesslike way for she feared she might disgrace herself, cry or stammer or whatever. One is not exactly a sight to gladden the eye, she wrote. She undressed and the woman reappeared carrying several things over her arms.

"Here are our models, Modom, in various sizes according to Modom's taste and with various stuffing materials, plastic, rubber etc."

Benita stared helplessly at the dangling bosoms, some small, some majestic, and wondered whether after all this might be the moment to indulge in her lifelong ambition to have a couple of tiny, sturdy ones, but decided against it because her friends might be amazed.

"We recommend this model, Modom," intoned the sales-lady. "It is filled with birdseed—it *gives*, you see! It has only one disadvantage—you can't wear it under your swimsuit."

"Really?" said Benita, and then, "Oh—I see—because of the seagulls!"

"Seagulls?" said the woman indignantly, "Not at all, Modom. They swell up in the water, Modom, that's why!"

It has always been a mystery to me that both Ronald and Benita Colman enjoyed excellent health all their lives, lived sensibly and moderately in a beautiful climate, were possessed of the means to consult—and did consult—the best medical opinion in the U.S., England and Switzerland, and yet both were struck, at about the same age, with diseases which apparently defied diagnosis until both were rushed to the hospital as emergency cases, he with emphysema and she with cancer of the breast, which, if correctly diagnosed, might both have been arrested in the early stages. One can only conclude that, while the medicines and treatments of today are superior to those of our youth, diagnosis has not kept pace. It is an alarming thought.

All plans for Christmas in California or moving to Rome were of course canceled to allow for Benita's convalescence, but in the spring she accompanied George to England, where he made another picture.

RITZ HOTEL
LONDON W.1

Friday

Darlings,

Yes, George is here. He only went away for a few days you know! I threw him out to Spain to try and get rid of a cold before he started this picture but he was back about four days later and brought me here with him. Billie came to Switzerland in the interval, and Juliet was in bed with the grippe, and no sooner did we get *her* up than I'll be damned if her friend Nicholas wasn't croaking on the phone for a doctor as it turns out that he lives just in a *bedroom* so I found myself carting blankets, pillows, soup, aspirin and God knows what around to *him!* It was all very unsatisfactory as of course I had planned to seize the opportunity to have everyone waiting on *me* hand and foot—or as Zsa Zsa says, foot and hand.

That Merle! I liked about the portrait best, I thought that was heaven. Anyhow I love to hear about people living in such silken luxury in these austere and ugly times and I think she is very clever to have brought it off—and rather lucky too, considering what a cross-patch she is!

How ghastly about the running tap and the flooded cellar on the night you left New York. I can see you both in evening dress at 3 a.m. rushing up and down with buckets—you must have been wrecks when you arrived in Mexico City! Tell Ellie I can't do those high places either. I felt frightful at Greer's ranch and I think that's only 4500 ft.

I do envy you going to Ustinov's opening, tell us all about it. Can't write any more, have to get up and go to the bloody doctor and then join G. for lunch—he's working in what used to be Londonderry House! Lots of love.

Benita

Meanwhile we had as usual leased our Santa Monica house and, after a short stay in New York and a visit to Merle Oberon Pagliai in Mexico City and Acapulco, had returned to Lausanne. I had for some time been anxious to have a frank talk with Ted Lowe about our friends' business affairs, and, his wife Pixie being in England, he was happy to come to dinner alone. In his cheerful way, he admitted that Cadco Ltd. was having serious problems. The Sussex factory, he told us, plagued by inexperience, inefficiency and total lack of management, had been forced to close. The employees could not be moved to Scotland and all had to be fired; the whole venture was a total loss! Meanwhile the construction of the huge plant at Glenrothies, wrongly planned and estimated, had ground to a halt for lack of money. However, he told me, Harris had found a rich woman friend who was prepared to invest in a large way, and he felt confident that with this help, and with the handsome profits expected from Harris' motion picture, the finances of Cadco would be restored.

On this last point, I could speak with authority, because it related to a business which I knew very well. There would be no picture profits, I told him, because they had no release, and without that, *Give My Love a Gun* would never be exhibited anywhere and would result in a total loss. Who had put up the money for it? I asked. He was forced to admit that it came from Cadco Ltd., but hastened to add that this had been done by Harris, and without his knowledge. I then

159

asked how it was possible, in view of the strict British Exchange Control, to get the money out of the country and into Italy? Rather uneasily he explained that it had been done through the Vatican! Finally I asked how it was possible that Harris should be able to do such things with the company's funds without the knowledge of his co-directors and, above all, without the knowledge of the company's accountant.

Upon this, he exclaimed violently that it was all George's fault! He had appointed an excellent accountant, a most reliable and experienced man, but George had insisted that if they were to operate in Scotland they must have a man with a Scottish name—and this man's name was Cohen. He was replaced by a Mr. McKee, whom George had found somewhere, but his name turned out to be no guarantee of integrity, for he soon fell under the spell of Albert, with whom he conspired to buy a costly twin-jet aircraft, flown by two professional pilots, in which McKee and Albert flew to Rome for gay weekends with the Italian movie starlets, everything being charged to the company, okayed by McKee. It was thus that the idea of making a motion picture had occurred to Albert; and McKee, seduced by the dolce vita of Roman life, had helped him to cook the Cadco books and get the money out of the country. In all, some £400,000 had been passed to Italy.

Despite this horrifying story, Ted still retained his optimism. He felt sure he could bring Albert under control, and did not think he should be removed as a director, because the company would then lose the £200,000 which his rich lady friend was about to invest. He expected an investment of several million pounds from the Italian government, with which they were going to build six factories in Italy. He had called a directors' meeting in London at which he would insist on replacing McKee with Cohen, and he was going to see to it that the finances of the company were placed on a proper footing. He had told me all these things, he said, because he knew I was an old and close friend of George, but he suggested it might be as well if I did not mention our conversation, either to him or Benita, as they would not like it.

My wife and I were now in a serious quandary. There was,

we knew, the possibility that our friends might resent our interference with their business affairs, which actually were no concern of ours.

A few weeks later we were in London. George and Benita were back at Weeks Farm, and we were planning to go down for the weekend, still wondering what we would say to them. Suddenly, we received a phone call from Switzerland which struck us like a thunderclap: Ted Lowe had been arrested for attempting to pass counterfeit dollar bills at Geneva banks!

At first we could not believe it, but a call to his wife confirmed the facts. He had visited three banks, but the sums he offered for exchange were so large that they required notice of the transaction. This had seemed to annoy him, and he pointed out that he was a prominent lawyer in Lausanne and gave them his name and address. An alert cashier at the last bank he visited thought the bills looked suspicious and phoned the police. Lowe went out to the airport and picked up his little daughter, who was coming in from London, but the police set up a roadblock on the Geneva–Lausanne autoroute and stopped his car. In the trunk they found about $150,000 in counterfeit bills. Late that night they brought the little girl home and searched his house, finding in the garage several hundred thousand more, some of which, it was said, were only printed on one side!

After languishing in a Swiss jail for nearly a year, Lowe was brought to trial and was sentenced to six more years in prison, to be followed by deportation from the country. The Swiss do not take financial fraud lightly.

The whole area was aflame with this sensational news, and clients from all over the world besieged the Roturman office in Lausanne, desperately trying to find out what had become of the money they had entrusted to Lowe for investment. Nothing was left; and most of them, large and small, were wiped out.

It was a bleak weekend at Weeks Farm. Benita, wracked with pain and worn out by the long trip, looked distressingly ill. She was stunned by the news about Ted. George, who had brought back from New York the largest and longest convertible Cadillac made, was busy in his workshop fitting it with two enormous reclining seats and a smaller steering wheel. He expressed little interest in Ted's fate, and seemed unable to comprehend how gravely it would affect him personally. We duly admired his work, which indeed was extremely professional, and I nicknamed his new toy the Chaise Longue.

WEEKS FARM

May 1965

Dear Brian,

The other day I was driving my chaise longue, as you call it, through a narrow London street when I was brought to a halt by a lady motorist who was double-parked. I honked my horn but she refused to budge. Traffic began to pile up behind me. I honked and honked, getting angrier by the minute as the woman pretended not to hear. Presently a policeman came up to me.

"It is an offence to sound your horn unless there is danger," he said.

"Well there IS danger!" I exploded. "If she doesn't move, I am going to MURDER that woman!"

The policeman was visibly shaken and went off to convince the woman that she should move out of the way.

I admit that there are times when my chaise longue seems a little on the large side, but I wouldn't exchange it for any other car. I just don't think Europeans know how to make motor cars. Benita loves the Rolls because it makes her feel grand, but it has the stupidest engineering design features ever put on a car and if I had my way I would drive it back to Crewe and throw it in their faces.

As to the matter of your Asian flu etc, I put it to you that ill-health is very largely caused by emotional frustrations, and conversely, physical well-being is substantially a fringe benefit of inner contentment, which in turn can only be achieved if the psycho-somatic system gets enough nourishment from its resting points of satisfaction. Unresolved ambivalences, especially in the realm of one's existential dichotomies, can spawn more diseases than unaided bacteria.

We are looking forward like mad to seeing you at Weeks again.

Love

George

The English press was not long in picking up the Ted Lowe story and throwing George's name into the headlines as a co-director of Cadco Ltd. His telephone rang constantly as insistent reporters besieged him for comment. At last perceiving his danger, and being unable to make any contact with Albert, he sent a man named Clayton, who had been hired to run Cadco's London office, up to Glenrothies to find out what was going on.

Clayton, who seems to have been a sound man, found that Albert had left Rome some weeks before for California, accompanied by a young lady whose expenses had been paid for by Cadco, and his address was unknown. A horde of creditors had gathered, and all building activity had stopped. After examining such books and records as McKee was able to produce, Clayton estimated that there was a deficit of over £630,000. He was so horrified that immediately on his return to London he resigned his position and went to the Board of Trade with his story.

The fat was now in the fire for Cadco Ltd. The Sunday papers splashed George's name all over their front pages, hinting at a gigantic international swindle in which he was implicated, and printing heart-rending stories of the distress among the poor people and local suppliers at Glenrothies. A question was asked in the House of Commons about the role the Board of Trade had played in supporting the scheme, and the Minister promised an immediate and exhaustive investigation. Finally the Royal Bank of Scotland, which might have been expected to exercise close supervision of the expenditure of its huge loan, now awoke to the fact that it was gone, and George received a letter demanding that he make good his personal guarantee forthwith.

With Lowe in a Swiss prison and Harris vanished somewhere in the U.S., George not only faced the brunt of the attack but also the knowledge that he had lost his money and his wife's too; and loud were the curses that fell uselessly upon the head of Ted. The most pressing danger, of course, was the claim of the Royal Bank of Scotland. George immediately hired the despised accountant Mr. Cohen to go up and interview the Governor of the Bank. It was a brief interview, in which Mr. Cohen acquitted himself well. When, asked the Governor, could the Bank expect to see its money? Mr. Cohen replied that unfortunately Mr. Sanders would be unable to make good his guarantee because he had lost his whole investment. He suggested that the Bank had been extremely foolish to accept Mr. Sanders' personal guarantee for such a huge sum without making proper investigation of his financial standing.

"Oh come, Mr. Cohen," said the Governor, "Mr. Sanders is a movie star!"

"I must tell you sir that not all movie stars are rich," replied Cohen, "and in fact very few of them have any money at all!"

The Governor stared at him in disbelief for a moment, and then he smiled knowingly and said, "Well, I understand that Mr. Sanders' wife is rich in her own right, and that she loves him very much. She will surely not allow this matter to proceed further?"

"Sir," said Mr. Cohen, "I must tell you that she does not love him that much!"

14

The Board of Trade investigation of Cadco Developments
Ltd., Royal Victoria Sausages Ltd. and Victoria Meats Ltd.
was conducted by Rondle Owen Charles Stable, Esq. Q.C.
and Horace Owen Coulson, Esq., F.C.A., and their report
was published by H.M. Stationery Office in 1966. It is a
model of its kind: literate, intelligent and exhaustive. Many
people were interviewed in Scotland, London, Lausanne,
Paris and Rome. Every pertinent fact was examined and eval-
uated with painstaking care and is presented with fairness
and clarity. As the many and various personalities involved
emerge and stand before the reader's eyes, one has the feeling that it could be used with hardly any change as a fascinating motion picture script. Its conclusions and recommen-
dations carry absolute conviction.

In reading the long and extraordinary story, we meet many
people closely concerned with it at various stages, of whose
existence we had been ignorant, and we learn many astonishing things, not the least of which is Albert Harris' villainy
and the way in which so many accepted his monstrous lies.
Starting as a penniless adventurer who had no experience
and was totally unqualified to conduct a business, he had
swindled the little Brighton butcher out of his shop and had
invented the famous story about Queen Victoria and the sausages. Nothing he ever told anybody about anything bore
any relation to the truth and yet, when the crash came, it was
found that there were no fewer than eleven interlocking companies in the Cadco group, in all of which Harris was a
director and largest stockholder despite the fact that he never
himself put up one penny. The investigators say of him:

It has been a matter of interest to us that of all the people who came in touch with Harris, those who, if they were taken in by him at all, very soon recognised him for what he was, were themselves people of obvious integrity, whereas those who were impressed by him, thought that he had a great future in business and who were not immediately disabused, were themselves people who, it can be conclusively established from the evidence before us, lacked integrity.

Of Ted Lowe, they say:

He is a man of considerable charm, but essentially weak, lacking the moral courage to say "no." He is by nature an optimist. He is ready to embark upon ventures likely to involve large capital outlays, with no more than a general hope that capital will be found from some source or other to meet the need when it matures. He is also a man who prefers to hope for the best instead of facing up to reality, especially when the reality is unpalatable. He obviously places a very high value upon what other people think of him, and is prepared to go to any lengths rather than lose their high opinion. In our opinion, of all those responsible for the state of affairs which our enquiries have revealed, Lowe is by far the most alive to the loss and hardship suffered by others.

Of George, they say:

Of all the people involved in the affairs of Royal Victoria Sausages and Developments, the person whose part has been most difficult to assess is Sanders. As soon as our appointment was announced, his solicitors informed us that he wished to give evidence at the earliest possible moment. Upon the assumption that, as a loser, he would be anxious to tell us all he knew and would indeed be anxious to have their affairs investigated, we complied with this request and saw him, with Mrs Sanders, as one of the earliest witnesses. His evidence was to the effect that he knew nothing about business; that he relied upon Lowe to look after his finances and ensure that he did not make any rash investments, and that he had been grievously let down by Lowe; that he had played no significant part in the affairs of R.V.S. or Developments; that he had no responsibility for any decision, had initiated nothing and did not know any details concerning the running of R.V.S. and Developments. . . . As our enquiry progressed it was established by other evidence that within three weeks of his appointment to the Board of R.V.S. it was Sanders who made the first proposals for expansion, by suggesting that Investment should build a second factory in Sussex and lease it to R.V.S. . . . We feel fairly satisfied by the tenor of the other evidence that Sanders was by no means ignorant of the financial possibilities of Government aid available to companies willing to set up business in Development areas, that he was present at a meeting where "the whole question of setting up a factory in Ireland with the Government grants which are available" should be investigated, and that it was Sanders who first suggested the Italian venture. . . . We attach considerable weight to his part in the early negotiations with the Development Corporation. Once the Group was involved in these negotiations, he played an active part in them, particularly when the scheme enlarged from one of £50,000 to one of £3,000,000. . . . It should be remembered that in the first draft of the press handout, which Sanders took no steps to have altered, he had been described as a trained engineer and a highly successful business man. Sanders was a party to this press handout which contained greater falsehoods than Lowe could allow to pass, so that he took steps to alter his copy of the draft. Sanders and Harris took no steps to have it altered and had it been left to them, the press would have been told in their official version that R.V.S. had three food product factories in the south employing 400 workers and that Robert Mitchum, William Holden, Charlie Chaplin and Graham Greene were connected with Cadco. . . . We have expressed our view that the whole Glenrothes project was a device by means of which its originators could recoup the very substantial sums of money which they had lost in R.V.S.

Sanders was a party to this device. We do not believe that had such a world-famous figure as Sanders not been associated with the project, it could have started. Sanders must be held materially responsible for the launching of the disastrous venture at Glenrothies; to have been substantially aware of the financial position of the Group and to have acquiesced, at the least, in untruthful statements calculated to give the impression that he was aware of, and perhaps providing, material financial support for the venture. We do not accept his claim to have been an innocent tool in the deceptions and even if his responsibility is less than that of Lowe and Harris, his behaviour was, in our opinion, indifferent to the point of recklessness to the truth or untruth of statements in which he acquiesced. . . . Before formulating our opinion on the role Sanders played in the deception of the Development Corporation, we decided to recall him to give evidence again, but the further evidence Sanders gave before us on 15th June, 1965, did not add significantly to our knowledge of his part in the affair. He did not substantially retreat from his former contention that he took no active part in the affairs of the Group, despite evidence that he had done so.

Of Benita, they say:

We cannot exclude from our minds the fact that Mrs Sanders, having invested a substantial sum of money in R.V.S.—albeit not an amount, we are given to understand, of major importance to her—as early as July of 1963, refused firmly to add to her investment or to increase her commitment by giving guarantees such as Sanders himself gave.

The investigators also say that in their view "The whole matter of the deception played upon the Development Corporation to induce it to enter into these contracts should be referred to the Director of Public Prosecutions in England and to the Lord Advocate in Scotland for them to consider prosecutions against Lowe, Harris and Sanders."

15

During the months occupied by this investigation, Benita's arthritis became steadily worse, perhaps proving the truth of George's assertion that "physical well-being can only be achieved if the psycho-somatic system gets enough nourishment from its resting points of satisfaction," of which my poor friend found none! When the report was published, she was outraged by its sharp attack on her George. The investigators, she said, had seemed such charming and understanding fellows, and she felt betrayed by them. George was only a silent partner, a sort of non-functioning director who was not responsible in any way; the poor dear had been swindled out of a fortune by Ted Lowe and now they were accusing him of lying and cheating and all kinds of dreadful things!

The dreadful man remained immutably himself.

WEEKS FARM

October 1965

Dear Brian,

Anyone who writes as good a letter as you do should learn to spell. It is not DISPAIR, but DESPAIR. The fact that you use the word so frequently is very revealing in a Freudian sense. The answer to despair is sympathy. It is sympathy that makes the world go round, not love, as the poets would have us believe. Love is all mixed up, and acidulated, with jealousy. Sympathy is a clear corroboration of opinion. Nothing makes one feel more secure than to have one's opinions corroborated. You have our sympathy now because it is undeniable that you are a helpless cripple. Your sprained ankle is the point at which all opinions converge in unwavering corroboration.

Keep it that way! Become a valetudinarian. Valetudinarianism is the secret of longevity and absolute peace of mind.

Love,

George

p.s. I am happy to inform you that I have succeeded in increasing my alcohol tolerance to three large vodkas before lunch.

In the following month, the American press reported that Albert Harris had been arrested in California on a charge of acting as front man at Las Vegas for a gang of counterfeiters, and he confessed that it was he who had shipped the phony dollar bills to Lowe in Switzerland. Harris and Lowe being both behind bars, George now realized he was in an exposed position. His lawyer advised him to leave England at once, and this he wisely did, flying with Benita first to Switzerland, where in a few days they concealed their assets, sold the lease on their apartment and stored their furniture, and then to New York, where we lent them our apartment in which to rest and catch their breath.

---

324 EAST 51 STREET
NEW YORK CITY

29th Nov 1965

Darling Ellie,

Here we are lying in your beautiful bed, reading your dear letter and eating your good breakfast!

I am thinking that if this house were mine there isn't one single thing I'd change in it. Your little lilac chair looks heavenly with that brilliant blue china and I adore your sentimental Renoir and the thin-making mirrors and the noble flock wallpaper and the colours, and the *comfort* of the living room. Really you have made it divine. What a lot of *things* you two have in all your houses! Beautiful initialled towels & bibelots & clocks & gilded chairs & chandeliers—I feel like going out and spending $50,000 to combat the feeling of being underprivileged!

We are going to Calif to Vee's house after all, on Saturday if that's all right with everyone. [Vera Bleck, the charming sister of Sylvia Ashley-Fairbanks-Gable, —B.A.] Helene produced the most fabulous dinner last night. She really is a dear, isn't she, and a damn good cook, but anyway we won't be in much and I'll see she doesn't get over-worked or over-wrought or anything.

How beastly if Ted is brought by the Swiss police to testify against Al in L.A. It'll probably explode all over our heads. Well, the hell with it, we'll go to Mexico until it's over. My God, the bloody business seems to have no end. I keep on reading in the papers of other people who are going broke in some similar circumstances—I'd never noticed before how often it happens. I guess there are an awful lot of crooks in the world. My dear, do you really think he would be handcuffed? Of course he will escape if he's not, and go and join the group in Las Vegas no doubt. I'm afraid Lausanne has an exceptionally lousy climate, worse than England actually because we had a *beautiful* October there. So anyway I imagine you'll be showing up next week one way or another!

We came on T.W.A. and all the wine is Californian and very bad, the caviar not worth considering and the food awful despite the magnificent menu card. However the flight was good and the landing featherweight which is the main thing.

Lots of love

Benita and George

It is a curious fact that both Lowe and Harris were imprisoned for passing counterfeit money, but no prosecutions were ever undertaken against anybody connected with the fraudulent companies. It is understandable that no stockholder wished to move in the matter of Roturman, S.A., first because it was a limited company with no assets, and second because the people who had entrusted their money to Lowe had solid reasons for not wishing their respective governments to hear about it. The lack of any movement against the Cadco group is more difficult to explain, especially in view of the Board of Trade Report, but it is possible that neither the Royal Bank of Scotland nor the Board of Trade was anxious to reveal its huge losses and to withstand the resulting publicity. Acting on the principle that what the taxpayers don't know won't hurt them, the Civil Service officials in Whitehall may have advised that the best policy to adopt would be one of masterly inactivity. Be that as it may, it is certain that the Report was suppressed, as I well know, because when I wrote for a copy I was referred to an address in Bristol, which did not reply to my letter. I then wrote again from the U.S.A. and was referred to a British Information Service in, as I remember, Vancouver, which referred me back to the Board of Trade in London, from whom I eventually received a card saying it was out of print. I am able to quote from the Report only because a friend in Switzerland had the foresight to order a copy in advance of publication, which he lent to me.

George and Benita flew out to California, first class as always, and stayed at the most expensive hotel as always. They later moved into Vera Bleck's little house, Vera having moved in with her sister Sylvia because her son Tim, while driving in Beverly Hills, was struck by a falling tree and totally paralyzed with no hope of recovery.

HOTEL BEL AIR
LOS ANGELES

Darlings,

Our servants from Lausanne are here with Syl and I think like it, although it must be awful there because the girls go from sleeping pills and bed and the hospital and don't see anyone. I don't think he can survive long in this condition, I don't see how it is possible, and of course the problems it presents—having to have a male nurse with him *all* the time—are just staggering. It's a nightmare.

How do you like that Ted Lowe! He really is a case! Absolutely barmy. O dear, O dear, how we do repine and moan in the night and wonder how we were so bewitched—worse than Oberon ever did to Titania.

I am getting very hotel-stir-crazy. It doesn't matter *how* expensive and deluxe they are, it's always hell after a few weeks and no piano and no books, it drives me crazy and then I was having an argument with myself last week and needed a Homer to answer myself and not *one* of our friends here had a copy I didn't realise we moved in such illiterate circles since Aldous died. Anyhow I finally remembered what I wanted, which was a good thing as I am much too cheap to have gone and bought a copy and left it behind!

We saw a lovely film at the Goldwyns called *Les Parapluies de Cherbourg*—*do* go and see it, it's up for some kind of award someone told me.

George did a panel show game on T.V. last night with that nice Carl Reiner and he couldn't have been more frightened if he had been doing *Tosca* at the Met, and it wasn't even live! Well, it's rather a relief to find *something* he's not good at. He's doing another T.V. next week.

We are seeing the Goldwyns mostly and its rather nice and peaceful, like the old days you know, a couple of drinks (that's *drinks* not drunks) nice dinner and a lovely movie after. Frances has been telling me the most marvellous—but *marvellous*—stories about Marion D. and W.R. and I have galvanised her into starting a book! Deb Kerr is here. So pretty. What a charming creature she is. Betty Bacall is also here, in fact she was on the panel show last night. We hear Jason Robards is a proper professional drunk which must be dull for her but she speaks highly of him just the same. She is very very thin and her face has become very big. I like her very much, do you? [Yes I do! —B.A.]

I must straighten things up around here. George plays that

silly croquet far into the dark. I think they are dotty, they barely get back for dinner!

See you soon I hope. Lots of love.

Benita

BEVERLY HILLS HOTEL & BUNGALOWS
BEVERLY HILLS
CALIF

Wednesday

Darlings,

I am afraid this may be too late to get you in Antigua, or is it? Your lives sound full of fun and frolic and treasure trove generally which I am delighted to hear. We are of course livid that you are not in residence here and miss you madly.

I am so malade I have become like George's mother, staggering about in agony all over and suicidally depressed and absolutely no good to man or beast. I think I have just about had it.

However that may be, Beverly Hills is still charming and we have been wined and dined and admiring everyone's lovely houses, and wishing George hadn't sold his, although apparently the taxes get more unendurable every day. George is doing a T.V. this week & another the week after next (*The Rogues*) and a narration for a very amusing Italian film, so we are pleased to be solvent after our recent depredations.

The Awards are upon us and as ridiculous as usual. Julie Andrews is nothing in *Mary Poppins,* and Audrey wasn't even nominated. Gladys Coop is nominated for M.F.L. in which she does damn all but I would be glad if she got it anyway. Chas Boyer says they have had to cut all her lines in *The Rogues* down to "Lovely darling" as she can't remember anything else at all—not that she ever could, do you remember San Francisco?!!

We dined at Zsa Zsa's splendiferous palazzo, she seems in great form, looking lovely and complaining bitterly about everything. Greer G. was there, she's become no end odd and when she greets you, you have the strong impression that she has just opened a bazaar and I for one fully expected her to give me a nice rosette for the biggest cucumber. Buddy did a few tricks, but I gather he is mainly preoccupied with awaiting a heart attack. Greer asked us to a surprise party for him: I don't know if she was trying to bring his condition to a head!!

I saw Veree Menjou yesterday. Pat Boyer had us both and Quique Jourdan to lunch. She is terribly melancholy but later on we spent the rest of the afternoon together and became very hilarious, though I cannot but think myself lucky past all counting in stumbling into George's path. Really it is past all endurance to have to wander about the world alone. I suppose marriage is not for everyone though: look how they *all* wanted to marry Sylvia, and God knows she did her best to oblige them, but I really think she is happiest on her own now you know. Veree said that when Adolphe was quite near his end she recollected that he was born a Catholic and wanting to do as much as she could she rather wildly summoned a priest—I think it was some unoccupied type of priest who was hanging around the Brown Derby, but anyway, Adolphe was in a coma when the priest arrived, stood at the bottom of the bed and remarked loudly, "He's DEAD," whereupon Adolphe shot up and shouted indignantly "I am NOT dead!" After a brief and rather fruitless discussion the priest then went through whatever rigmarole they do although he was clearly shaken by the whole thing, which was proved when on his departure he reached the front door and explained in trumpeting tones to the maid, "He scared the HELL out of me!"

Collier Young has married again, such an odd little creature. She looks like a mouse. The Lavender Hill Mob is making a picture with Roz Russell and Bill is very pleased with himself. Roz plays a nun. I am already planning not to go. *The Greatest Story on Earth* is called the lousiest film on earth and everyone says it's absolute hell. There's a new girl called Virna Lisi who is with Jack Lemmon in *How to Murder Your Wife* and I think she is the greatest beauty to appear for years. Italian.

Ruth Esmond and Glynis are coming to lunch so I must get cracking.

Lots of love to both

Benita

1194 DARLINGTON AVENUE
BRENTWOOD, L.A. 49

Sunday

Darlings,

Are you back in N.Y.? And were you in time for the black-out? The smog here has been indescribable. Even the street lights don't shine any more at night. I'm sure that eventually it is going to kill off the entire population. We're now in-stalled in Vee's little house which I may say is quite a change from the Aherne palazzos & George has been tearing around fixing the lights while I have been—unsuccessfully—trying to find a whole set of anything and wondering how a set of 6 single sheets can spin out over two beds, one double. Ah me! Well poor Vee has enough troubles God knows, and Basil had a heart attack besides and then went on a colossal binge and only sobered up, as British vice-consul, to receive the Snowdons!

The maid we have gets $80 a week, comes at 12 and leaves at 4. I'll be damned if I understand how people make out—and when I say people I do mean us! I am hating it this time so far, but the fact is that I am at my very worst in a rented house with no help and arthritis. One can't even have any-one to dinner because even if one hires a cook there really aren't any dishes to serve anything on. Vera sent us the most marvellous orchid plant after we had had to put in a new disposal but I must say I would have much preferred some butter knives and vegetable dishes which I am sure would have been a lot cheaper! Well, you can readily see that I am on a jag of bitter complaints! Rotted no doubt by the comfort of our homes and yours.

The rain is coming down in block-busters!

Benita

Saturday

Darlings,

We have had two sumptuous letters from you. The one from Ellie had been in the letter box for a *week* owing to the fact that it was concealed by greenery in the front and by a table inside, and we didn't know of its existence until Sylvia told us, and then it yielded up all sorts of treasures.

All the news of Ted induces a feeling of straight anguish in me. He has been like a terrible disease in our lives. What will Martha do at the end of ten years? It is a long time to wait for somebody she hates, even for the pleasure of pouring her vitriolic pity on him. It is a winter of discontent here. George is engulfed in depression and there has been *eleven inches* of rain since our arrival. It stopped yesterday, thank God. The domestic situation, combined with this boring, endless arthritis particularly in my feet, makes life nightmarish. The kitchen has damn-all in it, the knives are blunt or non-existent, no bowls to mix anything and not enough shelves, but a very large *mirror* on one wall!! After which wail of misery I will stop.

Zsa Zsa tells me that Jolie suddenly contracted arthritis in her legs which was a calamity because she couldn't dance (sic). However she was cured by a Viennese in New York and you will be relieved to hear she is now dancing once more. I can't write any more because I have to ask Syl to take me to the market. O I *do* wish you were here Ellie. I think I'll make a risotto and see if it conjures you up!

We knew about Linlithgow and the sheriff, and while I don't in the least blame him— on the contrary—it occurs to me that these disgusting messes result in *every*one doing the most awful things. Did you read the piece in the Daily Mail about all the authors going to sue Ted? With all those marvellous clients pouring money into the company I'll *never* understand where it all went to. Are you going to write him a note?

Here is Sylvia.

Heaps of love to both,

Benita

p.s. The poor Boyers are being so brave about their boy, but of course are utterly undone and Charles looks suddenly like a little old man. The other disaster area, Tim Bleck, remains too awful to contemplate. Don't know how they survive.

1194 DARLINGTON AVENUE
BRENTWOOD, L.A. 49

Friday 13th

Darling Brownhen & Elly, wherever you are,

Thanks for a glorious letter—which gave us strong Montolivet nostalgia—on your incredible birthday. I don't know how we all got up here in the geriatric group. It's a terrible business. I think the thing is to start going on LSD and stick with it. I can't see any merit in reality after 60.

I long to be at Weeks in May and am already suffering to think the apple blossom is out and I'm not there to wonder at it. The trip to Mexico is shelved for the moment as it turns out the only plane to Acapulco leaves at 9.00 a.m. and we have so far been unable to form a plan which makes such an inconsiderate demand on us feasible. I am rather relieved since I feel about as mobile as a Steinway grand and the mere thought of all those promenades at the airport turns me faint with apprehension.

We have bought a dinky little house in Brentwood but I'm not doing anything to it as I can't believe we shall be long in it. There is no doubt in my mind that I feel a consonance with Europe which I *don't* here, much as I like America. Perhaps it is that one needs more money than we have, though I do believe nobody, or almost nobody here has as much as they appear to or one imagines.

We had dinner with Rex and Hazel to see the Awards. Isn't her house simply lovely! He was absolutely *beastly* to her and she was on the phone next day complaining bitterly about her lot. I *don't* understand how people form these perfectly horrid relationships and then pursue them relentlessly as if they were the very joy of their existence.

George has gone off to have lunch at Walt Disney's in a condition of such paralysing elegance, and his face curled into such an exquisite sneer, as you never saw. Oh dear, I do wish all this disaster hadn't come about to make him so unhappy. I suppose Bunny takes the view that G. is responsible for not knowing what was going on. ["Bunny" was our mutual and closest friend, Mrs. Nigel Bruce, who refused throughout to accept George as a suitable husband for Benita, refused to visit Weeks Farm, and thus restricted her meetings with Benita to an occasional lunch together in London, which was sad for both of them. —B.A.] The thing was that it was explicitly understood that George's position was entirely non-executive, and he made it clear that he was both unwilling and incapable of playing any part involving the business—a situation which suited our crooked associates just fine as it turned out. The whole thing hinged on our implicit—and lunatic—trust in Ted. Even now I find it hard to believe that he was so utterly crooked from the very beginning. I wouldn't be surprised if "non-executive" was a contradiction in terms invented by Ted, although it does seem to me that a lot of people *are* on boards of things with which they have no active interest.

Those divine Swiss wild narcissus arrived and you can't believe what pleasure they are giving us! Coming as fresh, dewy buds, they opened flat out and you can smell them all over the house, isn't it marvellous they should last the journey like that! Thank you darling, that was jolly sweet of you.

We still talk about Mexico—usually around dinner time! I am thinking of writing an article on the traumatic experience of cooking a chicken, or How I Found Van Gogh's Ear Inside My Roaster. Have you ever encountered those *frightful* little parcels they put inside the bird? A sinister joke to destroy one's nerve.

George says Jean Negulesco is rather bucked, I can't remember what has happened, but anyhow things have started to go right for him which I know you will be pleased to hear.

Mike Romanoff got picked up for drunk driving, which he wasn't—drunk I mean—and the police beat him up. Abso-

lutely scandalous I think, but George says it was his own
fault for being un-co-operative.

Lots and lots of love to both,

Benita

Meanwhile, from his sanctuary in California, George was
not idle in his own defense, as the following letter shows,
although it will be seen that, as in the scandalous Husan Ltd.
affair, he displays no concern whatever for the losses of others, whether stockholders, employees in Brighton and Glenrothies, or the many local people—suppliers, construction
workers and so on—who had been ruined.

---

159 MEDIO DRIVE
LOS ANGELES 49

Jan. 1966

Dear Brian,

Ted Lowe is at Terminal Island Prison having been flown
there with a Swiss security officer and handed over to the
American police. He is sitting there, in chains I hope, with
a crowd of prostitutes and felons in 90° temperature and
humid smog. He was brought here to testify at the trial of
Albert Harris whose defence has been taken over by the
flamboyant Melvin Belli who made such an ass of himself
defending Lee Oswald's assassin.

As for me, every day is a struggle. Benita seems a little
better and in good spirits but my own morale is low. I am
sort of punch-drunk. The thought of having to re-build my
whole situation from scratch weighs heavily upon me, and I
wonder if it is worth it, whether there is any point in it. I
have no confidence in any of my decisions, since my life
seems to have been characterised by one piece of foolishness
after another, and there is no reason to suppose that it won't
go on this way. Anyhow, to bring you up to date:—

I have once more emigrated to the United States. The U.S. is my new "Domicile of choice." Switzerland has gone with the wind, and the wind was Theodore Lowe. Benita is still a non-resident alien with European domicile. I have done this because I find that California law offers the best protection anywhere for people in my predicament. I have bought a house which I can exempt from seizure under the "Homestead Act," which was passed many years ago to encourage immigration into the State. I am also allowed to exempt all my furniture, and enough money to support my family, if invested in Federal Savings, and insurance, and suitable means of conveyance—which probably meant a horse and buggy in the old days, but now covers my Chaise Longue which has been shipped here. I can now negotiate with my creditors *from a position of strength*. I hope to be able to make a settlement and avoid the necessity of filing a petition for discharge in bankruptcy, but if the creditors don't agree, I shall go ahead and file, and they'll get nothing. The legal procedure here is a sort of private and informal one which has no stigma and no publicity. So we shall see. The trouble is that all this is draining me emotionally to the point where I feel like a wet dish-cloth. But to this thought I hold with firm persistence: "The last results of wisdom stamp it true, he only earns his freedom and existence, who daily conquers them anew."

Love

George

P.S. Well cor strike the crows!

Love

Benita.

The bankruptcy proceedings were duly filed and executed, though it was never quite clear if the Royal Bank of Scotland and the other creditors were aware of them. The main thing was that George, from his position of strength, had conquered his creditors, and the British Government had defrauded the taxpayers, without any action being taken against either.

Los Angeles
January 1966

Dear Brian,

We have just got your rather gloomy letter. You put your finger on the crux of the problem—an occupation! That is what one needs, and I have gone broke trying to find one. A steady occupation which is concerned with life and progress. Golf, on which you seem to depend, is not an occupation; it is a pastime. Retired people use it to pass the time while they are waiting for death. I do not call acting a real occupation because it is too sporadic; every engagement comes to an end sooner or later and then a new occupation must be sought, and the new engagement will never be quite the same as the one you have completed. You cannot put brick upon brick and stand back and view the result and then put on more bricks etc. But to do this one must have special skills and capabilities which life has shown me quite clearly that I, for one, do not possess.

I am almost ready to give up entirely and do what the French builder did at Fréjus, when his business was washed away in the dam-burst. He put twenty five pounds of dynamite in his car, took his wife with him for a drive to the top of the hill, and then blew himself up in a tremendous explosion which rocked the neighboring cities along the Riviera. I would like to go one better and borrow an H. bomb. *Then* they'll be sorry!

Love

George

It would indeed have taken an H-bomb to make anybody feel sorry for him at this point. Benita's love and ironclad loyalty, and my inexplicable friendship, were the only rocks that emerged from the raging sea of unpopularity that surrounded him. Financially, however, he was as usual sustained by that scorned but steady wooer whose name was Show Business. He was much in demand for television appearances, astonishing the viewers by singing and playing the piano with grace, authority and genuine talent. He also acted in a Hollywood picture, and wrote me a note from the set saying:

Dear Brian,

Have you ever worked with Laurence Harvey? I have whiled away the waiting time in my dressing room by composing the following:

> "Hark to the tale of young know-it-all Larry
> A cross between Shakespeare and Madame Du Barry.
> With the vices of both, and the virtues of neither,
> He says to the world, 'You may have me as either'! "

Love

George

---

159 MEDIO DRIVE
LOS ANGELES 49

Jan 9

Darlings,

What a *glorious* letter! We fell upon it with our usual gluttonous delight! I haven't written with the season's greetings before—and thank you for yours, sweet and welcome—because we have been so dizzy as a result of our recent depredations that I became quite incapable of prolonged coherence without vagrant thoughts straying through my mind, distracting it with like say Ted's house falling down on him, or Al's face framed becomingly by huge iron bars—to which he is apparently distressingly accustomed. However we are now greatly recovered and talking to people confidently about the weather and such-like restorative topics.

All your news is *enthralling!* How splendid you are doing *two* obviously delightful plays! I think it's *great* and envy you from the bottom of my heart—and besides doing one in Florida at this time of the year and with dear Claudette is about as comfortable as acting can get. It's fine news. You're a wonderful actor, so act then and bravo! [Alas it was not so fine, for both were flops. The Florida one was a tryout and never got beyond Palm Beach, and the other, in London with Dame Edith Evans, was such a disaster that I hardly dared to show my face in the Garrick Club for some time after. —B.A.]

And you have taken the Amyots' divine apartment in Vevey! Well I'm damned! Of course you'll adore it. I can see it all. You, Ellie, will make it superb. All the boats on the Lake will converge on Vevey for your soirées, the Quai is all lit up, the Hotel Trois Couronnes is bulging with your guests. Grand pianos are ringing out. The Queen of Spain and the monarchs of Monaco are arriving to curtseying crowds in the square. Garbo is gate-crashing and Merle will leave her husband and have her face lifted—again—to attend your latest assembly. Oh my dear, it's going to be a riot!

Mind you, I suffer with you about a London house. It is hell, but I must tell you that every day I bump into someone else who has had to leave because the taxes are insupportable. We want madly to go back too, but what to do? It's not enough to give all one's money to the Government but, en plus, to a Government of which one has only the lowest opinion—it's very frustrating.

Yes I knew Farrow was bust but it would take more than that to shake Maureen's marvellous, impudent sort of courage which I admire so much. I once asked her if she was much tormented after the operation for cancer of the throat. "Oh that!" she said contemptuously. "I never think about it!"

Must stop now and give George a chance.

Love

Benita

Dear Brian

The solution to your problem is poverty. You must lose all your money. You and Eleanor have too much freedom of choice. When you're in Florida you must drive across the peninsula to Tampa and St Petersburg and watch the oldsters playing shuffleboard. They seem to be quite happy. They have no problems. They have no choice. They are not cursed with money or talent.

Love

George

I don't remember what the problems were to which George refers. The main problem with our long and valued friendship was that we so rarely got to see each other, and considering that my wife and I had moved our lives from California to Switzerland—with all the thought, labor and expense, not to mention the courage, that entailed—it was sad for the four of us that our arrival there should have more or less coincided with their departure. I cannot help feeling that it was George's restless nature and his constant efforts to change his life situation, dragging Benita with him, that were the root causes. It seemed to me that he was constantly throwing bricks, gift-wrapped, through the glass windows which he himself had constructed, thus exposing himself to the bitterly cold winds of chance.

However, it must be realized that without these long separations there would have been no correspondence. The famous letters of Madame de Sévigné, Lady Mary Stuart Wortley and others were written at a time when there was no telephone or telegraph and no organized postal service, so that they had either to be sent by hand or entrusted to the drivers of coaches, and they have come down to us only because the recipients preserved them, as I have preserved these and even then it was only chance that brought about their publication. In my opinion, Benita's letters deserve to be ranked with those of either of the ladies I mention, and I am content to let them tell this sad, eventful story. In doing so, I have thought it right to retain her English spelling, rather than change it to American, but her failure to date them makes it difficult to present them in narrative form.

16

In November 1966 there was a sudden and most unexpected change in their lives. George received a very attractive theatrical offer which sent them off post haste to New York.

A musical comedy had been written based upon the Kaufman-Hart play *The Man Who Came to Dinner*, and the management wanted George for the lead, Sheridan Whiteside, a character resembling Alexander Woollcott, the celebrated critic, author, wit and enthusiastic croquet player. The show was to be named *Sherry*, a lot of money was invested in it and the part was ideal for George, who forgot his strictures on the theater when he thought of the princely terms which were offered to him.

---

876 PARK AVENUE
APT 7N
NEW YORK CITY

Darlings

As you see, we have arrived in New York and it is all rather exciting. I don't much like this apartment but George does and that is the main thing: besides I don't think a woman is *able* to like someone else's place—except yours, and I must say I simply *love* yours—but as a rule practically everybody's decoration maddens me! At any rate, there's a big sitting room and a good Steinway which is very useful. [It was hideous, uncomfortable and gloomy. —B.A.]

We've rented the Calif house—rather well—for two years unfurnished and we think she may buy it. We don't much want to go back to Calif. It's *so* smoggy and having no servants is really rough I find, in fact unendurable.

George hasn't started rehearsals on the stage yet but is working with "the boys" on the songs here. His voice is really lovely and floats out like yards of blue velvet. R.C.A. has bought $350,000 into the show on the strength of George, the score and the recording rights. They wanted the whole $500,000 but the last $150,000 is already taken, so I suppose this must be regarded with a good measure of enthusiasm— not of course that it has any bearing on public reaction but it is an encouraging start.

I *do* wish you were here Ellie, there are so many things you could tell me, where I can get a vitamin shot and some fish and the best florist and a masseuse and all that class of thing, and we could go to Bloomingdales and find God knows what.

George went off to Calif today for two days, absolutely beastly it is, but he has to appear in Court for this bankruptcy thing and then—I hope—that is the end of it.

I am going out on the town with the adorable lyric writer on the show and his Chinese girl friend. Very exotic, these New Yorkers.

Lots of love

Benita

BEVERLY HILLS HOTEL
CALIF

Dear Brian,

There is not much in your last letter that I can thank you for. It depressed me. Nothing hurts like the truth.

It is not only in matters of business that I am silly.

I am a very silly man. Period.

If this knowledge provides you with satisfaction instead of quiet pity, then by all means be my guest.

I cannot follow your advice and give up my war just because I have lost a few battles. For the moment I have retreated to fight again another day. When I announced my decision to become an actor, everyone advised me to stick to manufacturing cigarettes. After they had once seen me act, they insisted. Now that I can operate passably well as an actor no one can think of me as anything else. It would make life much simpler if I could be content with my profession, if I could find within its confines the opportunities for creative satisfaction that I need and seek.

I don't suppose I shall win my war, yet I think it is better to die sword in hand in the attempt. I may present you the spectacle of a rather silly soldier missing his adversaries with every clumsy swing of his blunted sabre, but stalwart, in good heart, full of courage and hope to the end.

Love

George

p.s. Don't forget that if *you* are happy in Lausanne it is because of *my* rainbow chasing.

---

876 PARK AVENUE
NEW YORK CITY

Nov 20th 1966

Dear Brian,

Your questions about the laws of Bankruptcy in California obviously spring from total ignorance of the subject and therefore would take too long to answer in a letter. You will have to wait until you come to New York at which time I will be happy to enlighten you. The sum reported in the press—$1,250,000—though, as you say, astronomical, does not include Benita's loss! This is just the amount of the claims and judgments against *me*, plus the $360,000 I have already paid off. I am quite happy however, meeting triumph and disaster and treating those two impostors just the same. Am now looking forward to treating what I am determined shall be my forthcoming triumph!

Whether it *is* a triumph or not will make no difference to our plans. I have rented the house in California to a widow, for two years, during which time I am hoping she will buy it, since we will not be going back there anyway, no matter what happens to the show. California has served its turn. I explained my long term plans to you on a couple of occasions but on each of them you started yawning before I'd got half way through, and so we changed the subject. Any time your interest in these matters actually prompts you to pay attention, this information will be available to you once again, although I doubt if it will be any less soporific.

Love

George

Evidently I was, for once, angered by the patronizing tone of this letter and must have replied sharply, because a few days later I received the following:

---

876 PARK AVENUE
NEW YORK CITY

Nov 26th

Dear Brian,

I can't imagine what I could have said to produce so violent reaction in you. Certainly no rudeness was intended. I tend to get rather irritable these days when my parlous financial situation is referred to since it only serves to remind me of my crass stupidity and negligence, and I suppose some of my irritability flowed off the end of my pen. I am trying to set aside the mental anguish I have had to endure for the past three years and cultivate an insouciant, "désinvolte" and flippant air, consistent with the part I must play in *Sherry* in order to restore my self-esteem and bank balance. All of my homes are riding on this play. It has a very good chance, and I will never again be given such an opportunity.

Or, even if I were, I would never again have the fortitude to take advantage of it. Not many plays are written where the star part is an old man, and an *acidulated* old man at that!

Another good thing about this particular play is the music (at any rate from my point of view). The songs are constructed in a way that makes them possible to be sung properly, as opposed to *most* musicals where the songs are just written as pretty tunes, and to hell with the singer. You just go out and find somebody who can do vocal gymnastics and falsetto it through, or to use a more poignant expression, "barrel-ass it through"!

Rehearsals start Dec 8th for five weeks. We open in Boston and play Philadelphia before New York. They are talking about spreading the opening over three days, which is what *Cabaret* did very successfully. This way, there is no pressure on the reviewers and much less on the cast. You are bound to give a good performance on *one* of the three nights and *somebody* is going to give you a good notice! Anyway we shall see.

But to go to something else; there is no AIR in this town and unless you walk it is very difficult to get about. I don't believe the place has any future. I believe that one day New York will wake up and find that half the population has died from asphyxiation.

Ethel Merman told us this joke the other night at a party.
SCENE. *A ladies lavatory.*
(Voice coming over the partition)
"Excuse me, but have you any paper there?"
"No."
"Well, have you any Kleenex?"
"No."
(Pause) "Well, have you got two fives for a ten?"

Love

George

It was a hard time in New York for poor Benita. Her friends were in California and her family in England, so while George was working on the show she was alone in a dark and gloomy Park Avenue apartment. The arthritic pains, for the treatment of which she refused to go to any more doctors but relied upon osteopathy and massage, seemed to have become very much worse. We telephoned from Vevey, begging her to have a thorough physical check-up at a hospital, and she promised to do so after the New York opening but said she didn't want to worry George before that, as it was a very critical time for him and he needed all the support she could give him.

---

876 PARK AVENUE
N.Y.C.

Tuesday

Darlings

We're very keen on the *La Mancha* thing for you. We saw it in the spring. It's in the nearly-round with all the drain-pipes showing—you know the type—but it was really mar-vellous and we think the part perfect for you, and for your voice too, George says to tell you (what *have* you two been growling at each other about?!) It's a nice, flashy, poetic part, rather a big singing bit, more operatic than "numbers" so you'll have to get cracking on the do-re-mi department too!

How lovely it will be when you arrive. I've used *all* your addresses Ellie, and today I staggered over to your physio-therapist and my dear I'm *so* much better this evening I can't believe it! So thank you, thank you.

Liz Allen came yesterday and did some of the duets with George and I think she'll be just great for the part and *very* attractive. Haven't seen Dolores Gray yet—the producer said gloomily "Well, she only has to take off about 200 lbs!"

I *knew* from the moment we saw the outside of your cha-teau that it *had* to be the best apartment in Switzerland. I'll bet anything it will be your favorite house and the others'll probably drop off like pollywog tails. Wasn't it lucky you didn't take ours! Now you have lots of room, adorable loca-tion, parking, service, my God the lot! Why anyone would live here who wasn't forced to I don't know. Over-priced, over-populated, over-taxed, dirty water, dirty air, and each speck of soot on the window sill is about the size of an owl, no transportation and to hire a car or taxi for five minutes costs $10—$20, theatre tickets are $10 & $12 [Now $16 & $18. —B.A.] it's simply a madhouse, and a largely black madhouse at that. I went to Goldfarbs yesterday and *all* the salespeople were negroes! Personally I think they have the wrong lot on the reservations. One wouldn't have thought *any*body could consider the Indians such a menace to society that they have to be so rigidly controlled. You don't hear of any Martin-Luther-King Black Eagle shooting his pipe off about his rights and wrongs, but the coloured delivery boys here would just as soon spit in your eye as deliver your parcel. And the *newspapers* here! First of all there are only two, one of which is a 5 lb packet of mud with pictures and the other a 10 lb load of the Times: both are almost entirely adverts. I actually think with longing of the little Lausanne pamphlet. I certainly think you are living in the right place. But if I sound so cross I daresay New York is not so bad at all but just my boring rheumatics make me think so.

George just called from rehearsal to say hello, such an angel he is—you're quite wrong you know Brian, in point of fact we have never had a cross word and considering that neither of us ever stops talking that seems rather exceptional!

We saw Claudette the other night, looking just the same and quite indestructible, also Doris-Vidor-Rose whom I wouldn't have recognised. She has gone a kind of light ginger colour all over, and where did that nose come from? I can't understand it, I'm sure it wasn't there before. Then I lunched with Anita Colby and some high-falutin ladies and she too is immensely changed. She's writing a book about the problems of being forty. FORTY! I gasped "Those are not problems, they're pecadilloes!" charming pastime for a delightful age. That's one thing about Europe, they haven't got this extraordinary obsession for people in their 20s.

Really I must stop droning on. Do buck up and come over. I have an awful feeling you are going to put if off, are you?

Lots of love

Benita

We arrived in New York shortly after receipt of this letter and were able to see them while George was rehearsing there. They then went to Boston for the dress rehearsals and opening, but we unfortunately could not accompany them because we had to fly on to California to take back our house from a departing tenant.

In Boston there was the usual chaos that attends the out-of-town openings of big musicals and we followed the saga by telephone. Cuts were made, scenes rewritten and re-staged, numbers put in and taken out—or transferred to another act, only to reappear elsewhere—dances came and went, there were violent arguments, and everybody was exhausted, being replaced, or having a nervous breakdown. It must have been a shattering experience for George, but I must confess I got a little satisfaction from the thought that it was educational for him too, and he might not despise the art of the theater so much in the future.

The opening night was a disaster! The local press lambasted the show and, having the prevalent prejudice against movie stars on the stage, reserved their most barbed shafts for poor George. The management immediately began to discuss his replacement in the leading part, and Benita, as an old pro, was inclined to agree with them.

"You know, darling," she said to me on the phone, "George is not really an actor."

In an attempt to conserve their funds, they were staying for once in a cheap and uncomfortable hotel, and one night, in the midst of their travail and being unable to sleep, Benita turned over restlessly in bed and was suddenly struck by an appalling pain in her hip. Frantic with anxiety, George had to dress, wake the night porter and start telephoning around in a strange city in the early hours of the morning for a doctor who would turn out and come to help. In the end, it was necessary to call an ambulance and rush her to a hospital, where X-rays revealed that her hip was broken. Her so-called arthritis was cancer, and her whole body was riddled with it. The doctors operated as soon as possible, putting in a new plastic hip bone, but they told George that, while they could patch her up and keep her going for a few months, the cancer would break out elsewhere and the end was inevitable. My old theater dresser, who was now working for George, phoned me from the stage door, and I spoke briefly to George, who was just about to go on for the matinee. He told me the bare and brutal facts but had no time to speak more. I think it was the darkest moment of his life.

Benita being now critically ill in a Boston hospital, my poor friend had no alternative but to accept the suggestion of the management that he resign his part. He bravely played out the three remaining weeks of the Boston engagement, a total of twenty-four performances under the most harrowing circumstances, while Clive Revill rehearsed and took over in Philadelphia but was unable to save the show, which closed after a few nights in New York with the total loss of its investment.

As soon as Benita could be moved, they returned by ambulance to their New York apartment, and one shudders to think what they must have suffered under these unforeseen and terrible blows. All their hopes and plans were shattered as the new life upon which they had embarked sank like a ship beneath them, leaving them adrift on a trackless ocean of despair.

17

We had to leave for California without seeing them, but as the winter weeks slowly passed we had long and anxious discussions by telephone. There was so little we could do to help them. What could they do? Where could they go? With George's bankruptcy just declared, being unable to return to England—moreover faced with the probability that Weeks Farm must be sold—no longer having any Swiss residence, their little California house being rented for two years, and without the expected income from George's theatrical engagement, they could not stay in the expensive Park Avenue apartment. With Benita's short expectation of life, the old ideas of moving to Mexico or elsewhere had become impossible. They had turned their backs on California, but eventually we agreed that was where George had the best opportunity of working and where they had good friends. It was decided that we should look for a small house for them to rent for six months or so, and with some difficulty we found one in the Westwood district which even had a small pool, and we hired an old Irish daily woman to work for them, because Benita was really incapable of doing much by now and George's impressive array of talents did not include that of housework.

Upon their arrival, we went around at once to see them and found Benita in bed, looking very frail but as always full of good humor and good sense. We tried to find words to encourage her, but it was she who encouraged us.

"Oh, don't look so woebegone, darlings!" she said. "After all, you know, you may die before I do! Could happen in a car accident any day, couldn't it? But let's hope not. Anyway, if I go first I shall be all right, because I have a wonderful doctor here, a dear fellow. He has already been over and we had a good talk and he has promised he won't let me suffer a lot of bloody pain, and that's the main thing that bothers me."

We chatted for a few moments and then I asked where George was.

"Oh," she cried, "he's in the next room." She pointed to an open door. "George, come quickly! Brian's here!"

There was no reply, so I got up and went into his room. He was lying on the bed with his eyes closed and made no move, spoke no word to me.

"Well, if Mahomet won't come to the mountain . . ." I said cheerfully.

There was a prolonged Georgean silence, and then he slowly opened his eyes and looked at me. "I am the one who needs sympathy," he said. "Because I am the one who is sick. . . . I am very sick indeed."

I tried to think of some suitable reply to this, but he closed his eyes again, as if in dismissal, so after a few moments I murmured some consoling words and returned to Benita, who was telling Eleanor how delighted she was that her daughter Juliet would soon be flying out from England to look after her because George was going to Mallorca.

Mallorca? At this time? I couldn't believe my ears. What on earth for? I asked. She called again. "George! *Do* come here! Brian wants to know why you are going to Mallorca!"

We waited for an answer. Finally a sepulchral voice replied, "What's the use of explaining my plans to Brian? He never approves of them anyway."

All too soon, we rented our house in Santa Monica and had to return to our home in Switzerland, but we did so with heavy hearts because we knew we would never see Benita again.

June 2

Brian darling,

We were so happy to see your letter at breakfast yesterday and we *adored* your advice to advertise Weeks in the Saudi Arabian Tribune!!

You know I am very flattered and touched by your concern —and darling Bunny's too—but I don't at all like to feel that it is so excessive as to cause downright distress. That is very wrong and absurd, and pre-supposes that I have cornered the market in mortality when of course none of us knows who may outlast the other, and in view of the fact that we are all advancing into our sixties it is well to remember that the rest of the world will not be stupefied to hear that any of our generation has ended their normal span. Bun wrote me a very amusing and stylish letter incidentally, which I liked enormously.

I never heard of the Clinique Valmont. It doesn't sound very endearing and I think it most inconsiderate of the doctor to be Siamese! Perhaps his scorn will galvanise Ellie into wringing off a few pounds. Oh dear, what a bore it is for her to have to wage this interminable battle. I always think she might get thin if she ate *enormous* meals at the table but *really* and *truly* nothing behind the kitchen door. I do believe that's where the weight goes on.

It's so lovely having Juliet here. You can't imagine what a marvellous cook she is, really it seems all wrong to use her like this but she doesn't seem to mind at all.

George is going to do this guest shot in Madrid soon and we think he should leave in a couple of weeks or so and go to Majorca to cast a beady eye around for our Hacienda Semana (Weeks Farm, get it?). Who knows, maybe he'll find something. I'm simply longing to get back to Europe; it does seem so *bland* here in comparison and for the last ten days it has been overcast, and you know it is the oddest thing the way all the brilliant colours drain off as down a bath plug and the place lies around like a hideous blanched and fainted

Frankenstein. That doesn't happen in England when it rains; it just looks like a tear-filled Constable.

I have to have my hair done now—I had it tinted which cheered me up, so I'm blonde again, much better.

Lots of love from all to both

Benita

10308 ASHTON AVENUE
LOS ANGELES

Sunday

Darling Brian,

I don't think you need "view our situation with such alarm" dear. I think you are rather prone to that feeling when any change is involved—for example, our marriage, Juliet's drive through the Balkans to Greece etc, I remember you wringing your hands! As a matter of fact, I think change does give rise to apprehensions in everyone to some extent, but to give you our thinking you have to understand we start with a totally different set of circumstances to you and Ellie. We aren't *nearly* as social as you are—anyhow, George isn't —and in fact I would say we are unusually self-sufficient with each other. After all, we didn't know *any*one except Charlie when we went to Lausanne and actually only made one friend whom we love—Mary Chevreux—during our sojourn there, so Majorca would have no particular disadvantages on that socre. Besides, one of my dearest old friends lives there, Vera Emmanuel and her sister Clare Sutherland —somehow I don't think you know them—and the island is full of writers and musicians, and there is Kitty Miller and all her lords and ladies if you want that, so I can't see any social problems.

I wouldn't live here for anything on earth. YES, the smog IS enough as far as I am concerned. Then you have the impossible taxes and the impossible negroes and *no* servants at *all*, and there is only very badly paid T.V., *no* pictures, you are 6000 miles from anything civilised, the hospitals are such that only people in robust health can survive their attentions

199

which is to say *no* service, black and very offensive staff and grotesque food. I am sure the doctors are great, but as they are impossible to see it is only a matter of hearsay, except for the bills which are not only great but gargantuan.

George sends his love (he is lying here giggling on the bed) but says he hesitates to write to you because of the "undisguised ridicule and supreme contempt with which you treat all his ideas." In short (he adds) about Majorca, we have to go *some*where to have a house and, all other considerations aside, Majorca is the cheapest, as well as having a mild climate and being within reach of London—and that's about the size of it! And we think you'll like it when your room is fixed!

It's terribly hot here. I manage to stagger into the pool, which is a life-saver, but there is no shade in that little patio which makes it uninviting. The Boyers' maid is on holiday and their gardener is sick so Charles is out on his little pointed feet putting out the garbage, while Pat is making dinner. They are leaving on Sept 11th and hot-footing it to Castelleraz, almost as anxious to get out as we are!

Lots of love to both

Benita

10308 ASHTON AVENUE
LOS ANGELES 24

June 15th

Darling Brian

That was really a marvelous letter, such bite, so madly funny, you really are a masterly correspondent! I felt I had to share it and read it to Pat Medina who fell into a fit—almost —with delight. See, I address this to you only because I felt I had to thank you for it. But from here on it is to both of you. Ellie, I hope you have emerged from your hibernation like a glorious and rested rose. I was *fright*fully impressed you stayed for three weeks, I only did two at Abano and felt I deserved at least the Congressional Medal of Honor for it.

You will be delighted to hear that our old Irish bag has just left, and tomorrow I have Rita (of Kent) arriving, bless her little cotton socks! George left just now for Rome which of course kills me, but I do *hope* it will be a pleasant break for him, he sure could use it. No, he *isn't* only great when things are bad, on the contrary he is really made for being happy. Well, of course *I* think he has everything except wings, and I wouldn't be *too* surprised to see a golden-tipped feather left in the bed either!

I just had a letter from Viv Leigh who tells me she has T.B. Isn't that miserable. Poor little love, nothing goes right for her any more.

Wasn't that a *thrilling* war? I was so enthralled to see that sonofabitch Nasser creamed! Of course we thought the Israelis would probably hold out all right, but my God—what a blitz! I have a theory they should ally themselves with the Jordanians who are the only people thereabouts with a *trace* of rational behaviour, left over from the British no doubt, and the Jordanians could benefit immeasureably from the Israelis, especially in agriculture and in know-how generally, to say nothing of the facilities at Haifa. Why, Jericho could become another Palm Springs! The Israelis would only gain one thing, but I think that would hoist them into being the greatest power in the Middle East and that is the confidence of the Arabs, who have neither ethics, sense nor vitality in their own states. I am sure Lebanon would join such a Federation, and probably Yemen which must by now be good and sick of the Egyptian capers. Well, I won't go on about it because I regaled George with all this only to hear—a little later when he was looking for Time magazine—Juliet say testily, "You don't need Time magazine. You've got Mum!"

(They could by-pass the U.N. too, which would settle everyone's hash! Between the foreign policies of the U.S. and the U.S.S.R. it's a wonder anyone survives. All those arms!!)

How long are you staying in London? I hear the party was a wow. I just talked to Billie. Oh dear, *how* I do wish I was there and walking about. I wonder if I ever will.

Lots and lots of love my darlings

Benita

11 July 1967

Darlings,

Isn't it too sad about Viv. I can't *stand* it. Can you imagine, I had two letters from her last week worrying about *my* health! I know she was bitterly unhappy but it's a wretched thing anyway, and so much younger than all of us. Oh damn.

I don't know where you are, but Billie says you were at Weeks the other day so I'm guessing you are still in England.

The smog is absolutely impossible. Solid as a sideboard. Breathing is definitely out—thing of the past I assure you—exhaling only is what you have. I don't see how there can be many survivors, seems to me to be completely shot. Can't wait to escape to Europe. This house is very unfortunate in its low class neighbours. All the young males congregate in the house opposite and play on *amplified* drums and guitars until our teeth rattle, the windows crack and we are getting fitted for straight-jackets.

George has found a house, next to Maxine's in Majorca. It has very little to recommend it in its present form but the walls are 2½ ft. thick, it being old, and it has *three wells.* I thought that very interesting as I have never even had one well so far. See—there's a lot going for you with a well. You can wish on it, or meet Rebecca at it, or lead a horse to it, and I think someone calculated the circumference of the earth in a well, though I can't remember how or who.

Oh darling, your wild narcissus arrived dead and mildewed, they must have been held up somewhere. It was frustrating after all your kind thought and trouble, for which thank you anyway. I am planning to come back with Juliet, the head cook, and Rita, the little maid, on the 31st over the Pole and am simply dreading it! Twelve hours flying arriving at 6 a.m. with a 2 hour drive to Weeks! Pure hell darling. George has arranged for me to have a bed on the plane, which may make it a little better. He is going to Palma to complete the arrangements on the house and occupy it if possible and Billie and I will go out later supposedly whilst he takes off to all over the place to make a film. I am still quite ill so it's all very "flexible" to say the least. I hope I never have to come back here again.

Lots of love

Benita

And here is her last letter, on which she only put "Thursday," but I dated it on arrival, at which time we were in Vevey. I was to write to her again several times but she was unable to reply.

10308 ASHTON AVENUE
LOS ANGELES 24

Thursday
14th July 1967

Darlings

I've just written to London and this morning your letter came from Vevey. You're a pretty difficult couple to keep up with. You sound very dejected. I feel like that too. There's no doubt Viv's exit is an awful blow—what an enviable one though. Talk about "To die upon a midnight with no pain."

So your London trip wasn't so great? I think it's marvellous the way you juggle with all your houses, and Ellie with all your lists and phone books—I don't know how you do it. George's tenant on Medio Dr is *the* most awful pain in the neck and we can't *wait* to get rid of the bloody thing and the plumbing situations which seem to arise every hour on the hour and are enough to ruin your disposition for ever! It's nice to have houses but the responsibility and burdens are terrible aren't they.

George was briefly up for that ape picture and he said "After all we have just gone through, I don't know that I am emotionally capable of playing an ape!"

Weeks sounds *so* divine, I do wish we didn't have to sell

it, there is something so poignant about it. This new Majorcan venture I do believe could be made quite heavenly, but I seem to be so awfully ill it's hard to imagine I shall be able to put it together or even get there at all. Well, its no use thinking about it really. I miss you.

Lots of love

Benita

———————

With an ambulance to the airport and a bed on the plane, Juliet managed to get Benita to England, where another ambulance took her to the hospital. The doctors after a few days let her go home to Weeks Farm, which she loved so much, and there she slowly died, gallant to the end.

18

I wrote to George, expressing inadequately the heartbreak that we felt. Here is his reply.

Jan 1968

Dear Brian

Benita did not want any of us to grieve for her, and we are carrying out her wishes. The mood here is one of gaiety. Billie and Juliet have gone up to town for a few days' frivolity, and I am off now for a glamorous week-end house party at Leeds Castle.

As you know, I have bought a house in Majorca and am shipping Benita's furniture there from here. I am also taking our couple, the Burtons, who are inordinately excited at the thought of life abroad. I have made a deal with Whitney Straight to buy his Ford Consul for $300 and with my little Austin 1100 I shall have basic transportation taken care of.

My tax situation in Majorca is non-existent! It has an ideal climate, an international airport only 2½ hours from London, Juliet has bought an old castello which she will rebuild, and the Chas Boyers are moving there, so altogether my new plan of life is very promising.

I go to Mexico in the spring to make a picture, but have to

pass through London en route, so I will stop and spend a couple of nights with you.

Luv

George

He stayed with us for three days and was his old original and amusing self, playing the piano unasked—unlike my other pianist friends, who always claim they are out of practice—giving me singing lessons, and seeming relaxed and seemingly contented. He had sold half his property in Mallorca (which he always pronounced with a "j" in the English way) to the Charles Boyers, and they had taken over his servants, the Burtons, a change which, as he pointed out, not only saved him money but would provide him with some good dinners and use of the swimming pool. As I drove him to Geneva airport, I ventured to ask him a question about Benita's death, which was grievously on my mind. Suddenly, to my dismay, he burst into uncontrollable sobs. I said no more, we drove on in silence, and by the time we arrived at the airport British reserve was fully restored on both sides. I was sad to see him leave, and indeed we did not meet again for a year, but our correspondence continued.

HOTEL MONTEJO
MEXICO 6. D.F.

April 1969

Dear Brian,

The only proper solution to any of the problems which seem to concern you so much is Government by Instant Referendum. Every voter should have a small electric box with "yes" and "no" buttons. The President could ask for opinion on any issue—should the nation invest $50 billion to send men to Mars?—the informed electorate would flash back an immediate response. Technically, this is feasible right now. Automated democracy might dilute the power of a lot of Congressmen—no loss to democracy in some cases. I am convinced that eventually the whole world will be governed this way, and we will be able to get rid of ALL the goddamned politicians.

Love

George

I have no copies of the many letters which I wrote to him through the years except my reply to this, which I kept for some reason that now escapes me.

CHATEAU DE L'AILE
VEVEY

April 1969

Well George, you are a clever fellow, as your creditors must be ready to agree, but I am a bit stupid, and it seems to me that there are many practical difficulties about Government by Referendum and I don't understand how they can be overcome. I shall therefore have to ask you some questions:

1. What do you mean by a Referendum? Do you mean a simple question that demands a simple answer of "yes" or "no," as you imply?

2. If so, what sort of questions? Are they to be on foreign affairs, national or international finance, housing, welfare, defense, education, health, trade, shipping, communications, labor, aviation, the armed forces, roads, taxation and all the other manifold branches of modern government, and do you really think that the average man in the street knows about all these things? I must confess I don't.

3. How is your Referendum to be conducted; by telephone, like the Gallup and Nielsen Polls? No, that wouldn't

do, because many voters don't have telephone service. By going to polling booths in their local districts then? But they do that already, don't they, and if you look at the California voting paper they are asked to fill in you will find it as long as your arm, and many of the propositions are quite incomprehensible to the average voter.

4. Most important: who poses the questions? Who phrases them? You say the President, but do we really want to give him such overwhelming power? Who else? The New York Times, Time-Life Inc. Walter Lippmann, N.B.C or C.B.S., Sammy Davis Jr, or you, or me? Phrasing may mean everything. Suppose the question is "Should the Vietnam War go on or stop?" Everybody will naturally push the button to stop. All right—but the rulers in Hanoi won't stop, that's obvious; why should they, and indeed how can they without getting their throats cut by their own people: so where are we?

5. What constitutes your "informed electorate"? Everybody of voting age or, as Plato so wisely suggested, only those who have reached years of discretion and who have had some training in political science? There may be justification for his idea, because we see at this moment the Western democratic world faced with financial disaster, one of the causes of which, we are told, is the failure of America to balance her budget and support a sound dollar: we hear one faction calling for higher taxes and lower expenditure, another for lower taxes and higher expenditure, and on the international scene the problems of money exchange and the valuation of gold are complex and grave: do Tom, Dick and Harry really know enough about these things to give immediate answers? My fear is that your informed electorate is likely to turn out to be merely an uninformed mob, and I haven't much faith in that.

There is, of course, nothing new about a Referendum: Hitler, Mussolini and other tyrants have used it and the present rulers of Russia use it, for it suits their purpose admirably. Everybody is required to vote, and only one question is asked: Do you confirm the authority of your ruler, or do you not? The average vote is around 97% of the total and the odd 3%, unless they can prove that they were too sick to turn out, wind up in Siberia or a mental institution. When France recently exploded into anarchy, and chaos seemed imminent, de Gaulle went on television to suggest his remedy. What was it? A Referendum. The question? Shall the nation grant General de Gaulle full powers to take any action he chooses! Within twenty four hours, he could hear the answer outside his window as the screaming, rioting mobs took over the city of Paris. He quickly abandoned the idea and did what he should have done in the first place, got an oath of allegiance from his top Generals and then dissolved Parliament and returned to the normal democratic process of free election. Referendums won't help France at this point.

I don't just want to knock you down old friend; maybe you have anticipated all my questions and have convincing answers for them. God knows the problems of Government were never so complicated, although at times as grievous, as they are now, so I will try to offer a constructive suggestion too.

Our English forefathers were the first to throw off the shackles of autocratic power and to establish a free democratic parliament, and our American cousins, in their Constitution, carried the ideal of democracy much farther; indeed the Founding Fathers established a form of government which relies, in fact, upon a whole series of referendums, qualified and protected by a series of brilliantly contrived checks and balances. When a citizen votes at an election, he participates in a referendum, whether it be for President, senator, congressman, judge, mayor, or town dog-catcher. They, in turn, vote on other referendums, and the actions of the highest among them can be checked by a referendum of the Justices of the Supreme Court. The Fathers had the courage to write down their Constitution, the first to be written in centuries, and a noble document it is too, admired not only by me but the whole democratic Western world, as opposed to the Communists. In my opinion, our best hope lies in making the Constitution and the Parliamentary systems work as they were meant to do. If we tear them down, as the students and the beatniks want to do, we shall only succeed in entering once more the vicious cycle of mob rule, anarchy and chaos, followed, as surely as the night the day, by strong-arm dictatorship.

I wrote the other day to Mallorca, as I had no other address.

Yours ever,

Brian

He did not reply to this letter, which I sent to Mexico City, possibly because he was occupied with a startling new version of an old plan. We heard on the grapevine that he was hotly engaged in the pursuit of Dolores Del Rio, still beautiful, now rich, and the uncrowned Queen of Mexico City. His plan, we were told, was to marry her, become a Mexican citizen, and then run for President!

Now here, we felt, was a plan worthy of him and certainly one which would produce a dramatic change in his life situation. I am afraid, however, that we did not have sufficient confidence in the outcome to start selection of our costumes for the Inaugural Ball, and in this we were wise, because he evidently failed to pull it off. When next he wrote, it was from Mallorca, and it seemed he had made other arrangements.

GENOVA

MAJORCA

Dear Brian,

THINK ONLY THIS OF ME—that in some corner of a crummy foreign village there lives, for the time being, that old shit-heel from St. Petersburg—Sanders. I had a glorious time in Mexico, Beverly Hills, New York and Westhampton, where I spent a week-end of croquet with the Westhampton Mallet Club boys, beating their champion in a singles match and generally throwing my weight about in the doubles matches.

I picked up a buxom Mexican girl friend in Mexico City and took her to the Beverly Hills Hotel where I had the Bridal Suite—just for fun—and have this to say about it: if you are going to Beverly Hills for *two weeks* it is better to stay for *one week* and have the Bridal Suite. One's whole appreciation of the place is different. One has a feeling of quiet triumph all the time.

I am thoroughly fed-up with the whole driving bit. I find it *boring!* I am in despair about the behavior of *other* drivers. In Mexico they won't even allow you the time to get out and pay your taxi. They start hooting immediately! I hate the angry faces of other drivers and their wicked lack of consideration. But what is worst of all is that there are *too many of them!* Frankly I only enjoy driving a brand new Cadillac around *North* Beverly Hills, and the Hell with the rest! Any other driving, in any other place, in any other car, and for any greater distance, is now a chore as far as I am concerned.

What do you know about the Rio Grande? You must have passed over it in your flying days. Is it navigable and attractive? It has occurred to me that I might transfer my residence to a comfortable houseboat on it, so that Alberta—my Mexican friend—and I could cruise up and down from El Paso to the Gulf, thus being within easy reach of the Studios in both Hollywood and Mexico City without being liable to tax in either country.

Luv

George

I replied that the bridal suite at the Beverly Hills Hotel might give him a sense of triumph, but would only give me a sense of inexcusable extravagance. I also said that the name of Alberta, in view of past history, seemed to me very ominous. I had just read that a gang of counterfeiters had been arrested in Atlantic City, where they had passed large quantities of fake dollar bills to an F.B.I. agent named Albert Harris! (If you can't beat 'em, join 'em.)

In January 1970 we were in New York, where I received a phone call from George. He was in Boston at the Massachusetts General Hospital, but would be coming down the next day and would like to dine with us. He arrived leaning on a cane and looking very woebegone. We were shocked by his appearance.

"George!" I cried. "What's the matter with you?"

"What's the matter? I'm dying—that's what!" He whacked the sofa with his cane and collapsed onto it. "They say I have deterioration of the cerebellum!" he groaned. "I can't have a drink and I can't smoke! I can't speak straight and I can't think! I tell you I am dying!" Again he whacked the sofa.

I was suffering from deterioration too, I told him, and it was all due to the sunset years, but he was inconsolable, and indeed he was in bad shape. He had been forced to turn down a very good picture because his speech was affected, and he knew he could not do it. He was convinced he would never work again. He left for Mallorca three days later.

This was a very low moment in George's life and it was fortunate for him that his sister Margaret went down to look after him. He had always been accustomed to spending some time every day at his piano, which he had shipped out from England, but one morning he told his servants to drag it out into the garden and there, with a heavy axe, he destroyed it. As Margaret saw the beautiful instrument being hacked to pieces, she tried to stop him, but he pushed her away.

"I can't play the damned thing any more," he cried, "so why should I keep it?"

GENOVA
MAJORCA

Aug. 1970

Dear Brian,

I have been waiting patiently for something to happen (anything), so that I could write to you about it. Well nothing has happened. I have absolutely nothing to report. How about you?

Both my sister and I are going to a local clinic for treatment of our various complaints; she for Arthrosis and poor circulation in her left leg, and I for poor circulation. The doctors in London said I had a stroke, due to grief, financial disaster, bankruptcy and all the other stresses I have been through. Here they say I *didn't* have a stroke, but a micro-haemorrhage of the cerebellum due to acute lack of circulation—a rose by any other name!—not enough oxygen getting to my heart. Will have to take up golf, as ordinary walks are too boring to be endured. It is okay for the moment as I can do a lot of swimming (the best exercise), but come the Autumn I'll have to get myself a pair of strong walking shoes. The struggle to stay alive is beginning to look silly. I think all the world's problems could be solved by a simple piece of legislation: total inheritance tax relief for Euthanasia Volunteers—plus actual bonuses for the heirs of senior citizens.

I have staying with me my Mexican girl friend, Alberta, who is only 45 years old and she likes to go out *dancing!!!* She is leaving on Thursday to go back to San Antonio to continue her battle with her husband over their divorce settlement. In September this battle will have raged in the courts for 9 (*nine*) years! It seems a pity to settle it now.

Am planning to go to California for a T.V. show in Sept, and back here for Christmas. They Boyers are planning to spend Christmas here.

It was W. H. Auden, the poet, who said that life is a process whereby one is gradually divested of everything that makes it worth living, except the gallantry to go on.

Well, screw the gallantry.

LUV to Eleanor

George

19

Early in the following year, we were soaking up the sunshine at our little desert hideaway, some twenty miles beyond Palm Springs, California, when, to our astonishment, we heard on the radio that George Sanders had married Magda Gabor the previous day in our local town of Indio! He had given us many surprises through the years, but none greater than this. I immediately phoned Magda's house in Palm Springs and George answered me.

Yes, he said, it was quite true; and after the first shock we were delighted. Magda is a charming lady, like all the Gabors, and she herself had suffered for some years from an affliction similar to, but more serious than, George's. We believed they could help each other and I said so. Dead silence ensued. Was he going to give up Mallorca now? I asked. No, he replied. And again silence. As always, it was left to me to keep the conversation going, and indeed I wasn't going to let it stop there, so I expatiated on the many advantages of the marriage. I said he could now be sure of spending his winters in sunshine and luxury, both of which were most important to him, and he could dress in his favorite costume—a pair of shorts and bare feet. He now had a swimming pool, a lawn on which to play croquet and no financial worries in his dreaded old age.

George heaved a sigh, and then said, "Yes, of course you could see lots of advantages."

"Well don't you?" I asked him. "Otherwise why did you do it?"

"It wasn't my idea!" he burst out. "It was all Zsa Zsa's doing!"

"Zsa Zsa?"

"Yes! I took her out to dinner in Beverly Hills and she gave me a big sales talk about how much she and all the Gabors loved me, and how much Magda and I needed each other, and she said they all have lovely houses here in Palm Springs, and how wonderful it would be to have me back in the family, so that they could look after me and all that!"

"But it's true!" I exclaimed.

"Well, it may seem so to you, but it won't work," he replied. "I'll come over and talk to you about it soon. I have to go to New York on Monday for a few days to do a TV show." With that, he hung up.

About a week later my wife and I, in dirty working clothes, were busy as usual around our little house, I plastering the walls with adobe mud and she painting the window trim, when the phone rang. It was George. They were driving around in the neighborhood, he said, and would like to stop and see us. Hurriedly we cleaned up a bit, flung chair cushions around the patio, filled the ice bucket and put out vodka for George, but we were hardly in a proper state to receive guests when he and Magda drove in between the date palms in a magnificent new white Cadillac, both immaculately attired in high Palm Springs fashion. The desert sunset began to glow across the sky as we sat down to talk, which is to say that George talked while we listened and Magda occasionally and tremulously murmured, "Oh, George—no!"

He had come to tell us, he announced, that this marriage was ridiculous and must be annulled at once.

"Oh, George—no!"

"Yes, yes, my dear. You must trust me. It was a great mistake and won't work for either of us."

Used as we were to his abrupt changes of plans, we were staggered by this one. Eleanor recovered first and bluntly asked if he had any money, to which he replied, "No!" She turned to Magda and asked the same question.

Magda's face brightened. She nodded and smiled. "Oh, George—yes!" she said.

Well, Eleanor asked, should he not consider the advantages of this, even if he was unwilling to consider dear

Magda's feelings in the matter? After all, they had only been married for a few days and that seemed surely rather short for two adult, intelligent people. Think too, she said, of the scandal such an instant divorce would cause.

"Oh, George—yes!" murmured Magda, who seemed stricken by the idea.

George regarded her impersonally, as if she were some wax figure we were discussing. "That's just the point," he said. "How can I be married to a woman whom I have to ask for money every time I go into town, and what is the use of being married to someone with whom one can't have a normal conversation?" As for the scandal, while he was in New York he had taken a lady friend out to dinner while Magda had dined out in Palm Springs with an old pansy friend and both the newlyweds had been headlined in the gossip columns the following day. "If we were not married but just living together," he asserted, "there would have been no comment!"

The poor bride was now on the verge of tears and we rallied to her support. This was not a nice way to behave to a dear woman like Magda, we said, whose only disability was that she had, like himself, suffered an illness, though more serious than his. Oh yes, he replied cheerfully, he had known her for many years and could assure us that she was much the nicest of the Gabors.

How would it be possible, I asked, to get a divorce a few days after the marriage, and upon what grounds? Under California law, he explained, provided action was taken within two weeks of the marriage, an annulment could be granted by the court. And the grounds? Quite simple. All they had to do was to go before a judge and both sign a declaration saying that George was impotent! "Oh, George—no!" wailed poor Magda.

There seemed nothing more to say after this. We kissed Magda, watched them depart in the Cadillac and poured another vodka. A couple of days later, we read in the local paper that the annulment had been granted by the same judge who had, so shortly before, married them in Indio. Soon after, having once more changed his life situation, George left for Mallorca.

20

June 1971

Dear Brian,

Your book is nothing short of a masterpiece! Hope you make millions with it!

Would like to bring you up to date with my own situation and will give it you in headlines only, as I hope to see you in London soon. As I told you, I sold half my property to the Charles Boyers. There were two houses there and they have the front house and pool. My sister runs my house. My grandmother's maid, Paulinchen, is still alive but bedridden. She can only grunt in Polish and she will be 100 years old in October. My sister nurses her. She also nurses my mother, who is now an incontinent vegetable.

Am telling you all this because I seem to be surrounded by age and decrepitude.

All my movies have been cancelled except one which was stolen by Curt Jurgens. I keep dashing back and forth to London, writing scripts and having story conferences on movies that will probably never happen.

Age is a ghastly phenomenon. How are you and Eleanor bearing up? It seems, as I look around me, that all my friends are either dead or dying.

I wish Paulinchen would hurry up and die. Poor Margaret, my sister, has done enough. She deserves a rest.

My own health seems to be O.K. for the moment.

Best

George

I had one more letter from him which, had I known it, was to be the last. He wrote from Weeks Farm, Kent, where he was staying with Benita's sister.

Dear Brian,

You say you are ageing in a physical sense? With me, it's mental. I am now an irascible old fart, deaf and intractable. "Good morning sir," said Burton to me the other day. "What?" I said. "Good morning sir," he repeated. "What?" I said.

I called my sister last week. "How is Mother?" I asked. "Well, it varies," she replied. "Yesterday we had a conversation for about two hours, at the end of which she said, *"You* must be my *daughter!"* "Of course I'm your daughter!" I said. "Oh, well then, you must know my sister," she said. "Of course I know your sister," I said, "she's my aunt!" "NO!" said Mother.

Well, that gives you an idea of my family situation. It really *is* the last mile for all of us. But the most extraordinary things can happen in this life, and I find it very hard to believe that latest thing that has happened.

My father and mother put in a claim against the then Russian Government *50 years ago* for compensation of property of theirs stolen by the Bolsheviks when they over-ran Esthonia. Incredible though it may seem, the Soviet Government *HAS AGREED TO PAY OFF* these claims! They total some £12,000,000 (twelve million pounds sterling), and the

Soviets are recognising half the claim, or £6,000,000 (six million pounds sterling), so my mother expects to get that much. I'll believe it when I see it.

Love

George

In November of 1971 I dined with him in London at the apartment of an old lady friend of his, hitherto unknown to me, who had taken him in while he was making a picture and was cooking his meals and looking after him, in the time-honored fashion of his lady friends. His mother and Paulinchen had both died at last, and his long-suffering sister, Margaret, had returned to live in England. His picture had just finished, but of course he was negotiating another. Meanwhile, he had sold his house in Mallorca. Was that wise? I asked him, for I knew that Benita had planned it as a haven for him for the rest of his life, and in her last days had done her utmost to help him with it. He insisted that it was the only thing to do; he had found himself alone there and his only occupation had been staring out at the sea, which was slowly driving him crazy.

Knowing him as I did, this explanation did not satisfy me, for I felt sure there was another motive for such a drastic move. Over coffee, I pressed him further and finally got the truth. It was the same old story—taxation, from which he had been free in Spain but unfortunately had no earnings there. In England, on the other hand, there seemed to be plenty of work offering in movies and, if he remained domiciled abroad, he was not liable to British taxation. However, as I have explained before, the law exacted certain conditions:

1. He must have legal domicile in some other country.

2. Income from any source must be paid to him in that country.

3. He must not stay in England for more than ninety days in the taxable year.

If these conditions were not met, the British authorities could declare him a British domiciliary and tax him accordingly.

George had once asked his father where he considered the domicile of the Sanders family to be and unhesitatingly the old gentleman had replied "St. Petersburg of course! And when the present troubles in our country are over we shall return there!" George had found this Expression of Intent very satisfactory, but he was by no means sure the British tax authorities would agree with him. His difficulty was that he now had no foreign domicile, or residence of any kind. When he had emigrated once more to the U.S. it had been solely for the purpose of taking advantage of the favorable California tax law, and once that was accomplished he had renounced American citizenship to avoid paying American taxes. After the sale of his Mallorcan property he was therefore technically a man without a country. However, as he still carried a British passport, the authorities were entitled to declare that England was his "Domicile of Intent" and to tax him accordingly on his income from any source worldwide.

As usual, he had devised a scheme to outwit them, and this depended upon the fact, which he had verified, that the ninety days were calculated upon a twenty-four-hour basis, which meant that if he slept in England, a day would be counted, but not if he slept out of the country. Now the parts he played were usually short and often spread over the run of a picture; if therefore he had a few days off, a weekend, or even a late call one morning he could, with the cooperation of the Studio, drive to London Airport after work, fly to Paris in forty minutes and return the next morning if necessary without losing a day. He could not do this from Mallorca which has only one daily flight of two and a half hours, leaving at an unsuitable time and liable to be booked solid in the tourist season. He believed he had solved the problem by buying a cottage near Fontainebleau, only fifteen minutes by car from Orly Airport. He had engaged an architect and was remodeling it at that moment.

I asked if he had any friends in or near Fontainebleau. None, he said, and he didn't want them. He was delighted to know that he would be surrounded by forest, where no-body was allowed to build. I pointed out that he could be occupied, at best, for three months or so a year in England and the rest of the time, instead of staring out at the sea, he would be staring out at the trees. I also ventured to say that it was time he learned that taxes should follow the man, not man the taxes. Choose to live where you are happy, and where you have good friends, I advised him, and pay what is asked of you for the privilege.

He looked at me and sighed wearily. Then he turned to his friend and said, "Brian never approves of my plans."

Early in March 1972 we were again in California and heard that George was visiting Beverly Hills with his old lady friend and her sister. I called at once and they told me he could not come to the phone as he was recovering from an accidental overdose of sleeping pills, but a doctor was in attendance and there was no doubt he would be in good shape in a few days. They invited us to Sunday lunch, as they were all flying back to Europe on the Monday and would shortly be going to Biarritz to look for a house for George. Biarritz? What had happened to Fontainebleau? He had sold it!

Memories came back to me of Lausanne, the house on the Yonne, Beauvais, the Bahamas, Beverly Hills, Mallorca, Fontainebleau, and now Biarritz—all part of his lifetime battle with the tax man. I thought how poor Benita would have grieved.

The lunch party was very distressing. He was drinking large glasses of straight vodka, looking dreadfully ill, and hardly made any sense. I tried to talk to him, but he seemed not to understand me. Suddenly he asked, "How many does it take?"

"How many what George?"

"Pills. How many does it take?"

"I don't know," I said, "but don't be a fool George. Look after yourself!"

"But I know now what is wrong with me!" he cried. "I never should have sold the Majorca house! That was my great mistake! Why did I do it! Everything I do is wrong. I can't do right. I must be crazy!"

I tried to comfort him, to tell him that was in the past, that he could buy another house, or build anywhere he chose, and indeed I had heard that the Boyers were willing to sell theirs, but he didn't seem to understand me. My hostess intervened, saying cheerfully that he would be fine when they got to Biarritz, found a house and started the fun of fixing it up. Aside, she whispered that she thought he was drinking far too much vodka, with which I could only agree.

That evening I called Dr. Theodore Rothman, his psychiatrist in California for many years, who told me he had seen George. I expressed my apprehension about the flight to Europe, and he replied, "It is madness. Unless he is put into a clinic tomorrow the end is inevitable."

Under the circumstances, there was nothing more we could do. It was the last time I saw my friend, although I was to speak to him briefly once more. I reached an important birthday at the beginning of May, and my wife and I decided to give a small house party for a few close friends at the lovely Il Pellicano Hotel at Porto Ercole in Italy. Of course George was on my list, but it took me some days to locate him at the Lancaster Hotel in Paris. I phoned him from Vevey, described the occasion, and begged him to fly to Geneva, where I would meet him and take him to our home for a couple of nights before driving down to Italy.

His speech sounded confused as he replied, "Oh, I know you. I suppose I would have to wear a dinner jacket and smoke a cigar!"

No, I assured him, no evening dress, no speeches and no presents. Just a few days' fun with old friends.

"I am on my way to Barcelona," he said.

"Barcelona? Whatever for?"

"To find a house to live in."

"In Barcelona?" I couldn't believe this one.

"Yes. It's on the mainland."

"But it's just a commercial Spanish city. You don't know anybody there, and it's miles away from anywhere! You can't live there, George!"

"Well . . . anyway . . . I'll think about your party. I'll let you know."

"Oh, do come!" I begged him. "You can fly to Barcelona later from Rome, or if you insist on going to Barcelona first, you can fly to Rome from there, and I will meet you at the airport. Now come on, you dreadful man. It will do you good!"

He gave me the old silence, a long one, but I stuck it out. Finally he said in a low voice, "I'm very neurotic now, you know. I'll phone you."

He did not phone, and he did not come, for he had an appointment in Samara. Four days after I spoke to him, we read of his death.

The passing of a famous actor always rates a paragraph in the world's press, and sometimes a headline. People read it with a twinge of nostalgia, for they have enjoyed his work so many years that they feel they know him; another light goes out for them, and they feel older. The suicide of George Sanders was disturbing to many, but there were few, I think, who grieved for him personally, and this would not have disturbed him, for there were so few about whom he cared. Personal relations seemed oddly unimportant to him; but those of us who do grieve feel deeply about his going. Our lives were enriched by knowing him, and we now regret that we could not do more to help him. Stuart Hall, always ill-treated but always loyal, regrets that he did not make a greater effort on that last tragic visit to California. Zsa Zsa, who happened to arrive in London shortly before he left for Barcelona, saw at once how sick he was and, always loyal and loving, insisted on taking him to yet another psychiatrist in whom she had great faith.

She relates that when George walked into the office he said, "All right, here I am. And now, as there is no point in wasting your time, I might as well leave."

"By all means do so if you wish, Mr. Sanders," replied the psychiatrist, "but as you have to pay me for the visit anyway why not stay for the hour?"

He stayed, but did not repeat the visit. Having done what she could, Zsa Zsa had to return to California, and she regrets that she did not take him with her. His devoted sister, Margaret, regrets that she did not insist on going to Spain with him. His lady friend regrets that she did not realize when she left for the South of France the desperate condition he was in. I, who did realize it, regret that I did not go immediately to Paris and bring my friend home to Vevey. All these regrets are useless and unnecessary, because during his life we gave him, individually, our friendship and our love, insofar as he would accept them, but—at least after the death of Benita—he strayed alone through the world, still seeking but never finding the foot of that elusive rainbow upon which his eyes were fixed.

It was cold and raining in Barcelona. He had expected to arrive unnoticed, but representatives of the local television station were at the airport to meet him, begging for an interview, and he could not escape them. Wearily, almost in a daze, he went through with it, answering mechanically the usual questions, and then he fled to the seclusion of a small hotel overlooking the sea. There, alone in a strange little room, he took out his bottle of vodka and his five carefully collected bottles of barbiturate pills, wrote two short notes, and then plunged into oblivion, changing for the last, irrevocable time his Legal Residence, his Domicile of Intent, and his Life Situation.